PRECIOUS
CHRIST

PRECIOUS
CHRIST

UNDERSTANDING
the MYSTERY
of DIVINE
INCARNATION

WORD OF GRACE
INTERNATIONAL MINISTRIES

Precious Christ. Understanding the Mystery of Divine Incarnation.

© 2021 by Aleksey Kolomiytsev

© 2021 by Word of Grace International Ministries

All rights reserved. No part of this book may be reproduced, stored in a retrieval system, or transmitted, in any form or by any means-electronic, mechanical, photocopying, recording, or otherwise-without prior written permission.

International Standard Book Number: ISBN 978-966-2640-76-2

Originally published in Russian language as "Драгоценный Христос. Постигая тайну Боговоплощения.", copyright © 2016 by Kolomiytsev A., © 2016 by Word of Grace International Ministries. First paperback edition: 2016.

Edited by Abigail Joy Huffstutler, Olga Melnikova
Translated from Russian by Aleksandr Fesenko
Original cover design by Igor Konyuchka
English cover design and layout by Olga Melnikova

Scripture quotations are from The ESV® Bible (The Holy Bible, English Standard Version®), copyright © 2001 by Crossway, a publishing ministry of Good News Publishers. Used by permission. All rights reserved.

All italics and bolds in quotations of Scripture have been added by the author.

All websites listed herein are accurate at the time of publication but may change in the future or cease to exist. The listing of website references and resources does not imply publisher endorsement of the site's entire contents. Groups and organizations are listed for informational purposes, and listing does not imply publisher endorsement of their activities.

Printed in Ukraine.
www.preciouschrist.org

 Word of Grace International Ministries

FOREWORD

> "But when the fullness of time had come, God sent forth his Son, born of woman, born under the law, to redeem those who were under the law, so that we might receive adoption as sons." Galatians 4:8

God has blessed me in tremendous ways while journeying His path of providence and I am especially grateful for meeting Pastor Aleksey Kolomiytsev at a missionary retreat in California several years ago. My years of working in Russia and learning the language, combined with our common love for the Word of God and the God of the Word, sealed an instant bond of friendship and an ongoing and growing fellowship in the gospel.

Aleksey pastors Word of Grace Bible Church in Battle Ground, Washington. Our meeting revealed a powerful example of the word of the Lord sounding forth in the Russian language originating right here in America.

Very early in life, God gave Aleksey Kolomiytsev a calling and a charge to preach the gospel. He grew up in the underground church in the Soviet Union. Aleksey knows the cost of discipleship and taking up the cross of Christ. Bibles were smuggled, reproduced, and distributed in pieces. Having a complete book was rare. Believers were denied opportunities in education and vocation. In Soviet times, church leaders had little access to educational material and no opportunity for theological training. The KGB actively pursued the leaders, and many were captured and served prison sentences. Some were executed. Aleksey's father, a minister of the Gospel for over 70 years, spent three years imprisoned for his faith.

After the Soviet Union fell, realizing his own need for theological training, Aleksey came to America and attended The Master's Seminary with the intent to return to his native land to preach the Gospel. The Lord had other plans and called him to preach in America.

Aleksey has pastored a Russian-speaking Slavic-immigrant church in the Pacific Northwest since 2002. His exposition of Scripture had an immediate and profound impact on the congregation, and a growing influence beyond. Early on, a few volunteers within the congregation wanted to make the recorded sermons available to those who couldn't attend Sunday worship service and did so through the church website. What the Lord did with that act of faithfulness and obedience is profound.

Through the website (later radio, on-line platforms such as YouTube, and a smart phone application), Aleksey's faithful expository preaching quickly grew in global awareness across the former Soviet Union and among Russian-speaking believers throughout the rest of the world. Via the internet, the number of worldwide listeners has grown across more than 120 countries to number nearly 2 million every month. Simply put, **Aleksey is the most listened-to Russian evangelical preacher in the world.**

Over the years, several sermon series have been edited into book form, with wide distribution to Russian readers. This is the first of those books to be translated into English and English speakers will be tremendously edified and blessed.

I first worked my way through the original Russian version of Precious Christ: Comprehending the Mystery of the Incarnation ("Драгоценный Христос. Постигая тайну Боговоплощения.") in about 2015 to supplement my learning of the Russian language. "This book needs to be translated into English!" was my immediate reaction.

That desire is now realized. Precious Christ will bring the English reader to a fuller and deeper comprehension of the person of Jesus Christ and grand purpose behind the incarnation of the Second Person of the Trinity. Rich in content and broad in scope, this accessible book brings sense to the tapestry of God's revelation found in the Bible and connects the theological to the practical questions of life.

With a pastor's heart and a gift of teaching, Aleksey leads the reader through the logic of God's redemptive purpose in the Messiah as revealed in the Old and New Testaments. He anticipates and answers the reader's questions along the way. Aleksey brings to light the profound impact of the truth of Scripture as it reveals the precious person and work of Jesus Christ.

Precious Christ glorifies our Savior and will edify you, the reader. I pray the Lord uses it to grow you more into Christlikeness, in time and for eternity.

> *Jeffrey N. Williams*
> *Doctor of Ministry, The Master's Seminary,*
> *American Astronaut*

With thankfulness to God for my parents,
whose sacrificial love for Christ
taught me to love Him.

CONTENTS

	A Conundrum of Cosmic Significance	17
CHAPTER I	The Mystery of Divine Incarnation	23
CHAPTER II	Born To Die	77
CHAPTER III	Born To Live	125
CHAPTER IV	Born To Rise from the Dead	159
CHAPTER V	Born To Ascend to Heaven	193
CHAPTER VI	Born To Save	231

INTRODUCTION

Christmas is mysterious and precious to everyone, yet for different reasons. For many people indeed it has more meaning than simply Christmas tree decorations, Christmas lights, and the music playing in stores. It has more meaning than the presents we give to each other. For many, Christmas is the celebration of the Lord Jesus Christ, their personal Savior.

Even for people who are far from religious, Christmas is a special occasion to disrupt the humdrum of life and go to church, even if it be only once a year.

Christmas brings families together. During Christmas, superstitious students are unwilling to open their textbooks. Even atheists do not prefer to work on Christmas Day. This holiday carries something special, a certain weight, and a core meaning... Christmas has a significance that has outlived many a godless generation, something that truly merits the beginning of a new era.

If we think deep about the true, biblical significance of Christmas, it is something so inconceivable, so grand, and so potent that we cannot help being filled with awe. Just think about it: God became man!

The effect these three words have upon me is similar to what you could feel standing on the ocean shore, gazing upon its limitless expanse as far as your eyes could take it in. And, no matter how far the horizon might stretch, you would know that the ocean is so much more powerful and bigger in scale than what you perceive.

This is the same feeling that overwhelms me when I attempt to come closer to Christ in my feeble mind, juxtaposing these two components: His divinity and His humanity. Oh, how great the mystery! Oh, how limited the mind!

Yet, in spite of the intellectual unattainability of this truth, the Holy Scriptures vigorously encourage people to dwell on it. God considers it vital that we constantly face the magnitude of this mystery.

As a pastor of a church, I have always regretted the fact that I managed to preach on Christmas only once a year. This topic is too vast for one brief church service. Thus, a dream was born to present a set of questions to the members of our local church and to all those who are at least somewhat intrigued by the meaning of Christmas: *Why was Christ born? Why was it necessary for God to become man? What was it that compelled Him to set aside His glory, limit His power, and shackle His divine nature within human limitation?*

As a result of pondering these questions, a brief series of sermons was conceived on the topic of the incarnation of Jesus Christ, and with them also this book, unveiling certain dimensions of the Person of God-Man, those we may be so used to hearing about yet rarely contemplate in depth. I borrowed the thesis for this book from the beloved apostle Paul, who gave arguably the most precise definition of the phenomenon of divine incarnation in one of the letters to his disciple Timothy:

> If I delay, you may know how one ought to behave in the household of God, which is the church of the living God, a pillar and buttress of the truth. Great indeed, we confess, is the mystery of godliness: He was manifested in the flesh, vindicated by the Spirit, seen by angels, proclaimed among the nations, believed on in the world, taken up in glory. (1 Tim. 3:15–16)

A CONUNDRUM OF COSMIC SIGNIFICANCE

In the instructions of Paul to young pastor Timothy concerning the proper leading of the church, this mature minister of God set all of the secondary and human-minded aspects aside, focusing on one truth that is key for the life of God's people — namely, the truth of the divine incarnation.

> If I delay, you may know how one ought to behave in the household of God, which is the church of the living God, a pillar and buttress of the truth. Great indeed, we confess, is the mystery of godliness: **He was manifested in the flesh.**[1] (1 Tim. 3:15–16)

This is the strategic point of the church's theology and ministry: to exalt the truth of divine incarnation with all of its life, preaching, and even with her very structure, securing it as if on a tall column ("the pillar of truth"), making it viewable to all.

But as years went by, somewhere in the history of Christianity there began to appear adjustments. Piled upon this column were the ideas of salvation by human merit; moral, economic, social and political values of the non-Christian world; the exceptionality of certain individuals, churches and nations. At times, fastened to the very top of the column were some hastily assembled doctrines, giving birth to one denomination after another. Sometimes one could find there quite sound biblical truths which, nonetheless, do not have a central place in Christian doctrine. As a result, churches have ended up as secular organizations, charitable funds, and missions.

Before we even begin to examine the essence of the astonishing phenomenon of divine incarnation, I want to help every one of us realize together with the apostle Paul why it is so crucial to pay attention to this particular mystery of the Holy Scriptures, and not another.

The act of divine incarnation is more than just a demonstration of God's wisdom, inconceivability, and phenomenal imaginative power. The reason why God became man was the fact that man was doomed. You and I were destined for eternal perdition! And God knew better than anyone how extremely serious that was. That's why divine incarnation is a shocking testimony of God's practical love to sinners deserving everlasting condemnation.

The people of the Old Testament did not know God this way. The verse recorded in the Gospel of John1 that has become so familiar to many Christians must have caused Nicodemus a pronounced ringing in his ears. It was an absolutely new, outlandish statement: *God loves the world so much that He gave the life of His Only Son to save it!*

Among dead religions filled with fear, prohibitions, uncertainty, or a sense of exceptionality, Christianity alone shines with its strikingly profound peace, purity, and joy. That is because knowing and worshipping a God Who loves and saves sinners is a pleasure beyond comparison!

However, salvation of fallen mankind was not an easy undertaking, even for God. It is, in essence, the hardest thing to do in the entire universe. If you try to comprehend how a human cell functions, how outer space is arranged, how the laws of physics and chemistry work, you will encounter phenomena of incredible complexity — yet salvation is more complicated than all of them!

To bring it to pass, a number of humanly impossible tasks had to be solved, and only God's intervention into human existence could have achieved it.

- This cosmic conundrum is complicated by the sheer virtue of the sinfulness of man. His sin is still there. His guilt cannot be stricken. Sin is a fact. In divine economy, in God's holiness system, man's debt of sin keeps growing, and it calls for action. But there could be only one course of action: sin must be punished. And to punish the sin of mankind with death while saving human lives, the **Messiah had to be born in order to die.**

- However, salvation requires not only the forgiveness of sin, but a completely holy life as well. Imagine that all your past sins have been forgiven. That very second you have realize forgiveness, you start generating new sins! Therefore, there must not only be a holy sacrifice, but also a holy life. It was for this reason that Jesus did not descend from heaven straight to the cross. He went through all the stages of man's journey from birth to death. He lived a perfect life so that it could be credited to you and me. **The Messiah was born to live!**

- Besides, we know that as a consequence of sin, all men are mortal. Salvation is incomplete by definition if death continues to reign in this world. For this spiritual equation to make sense, one persistent variable had to be removed. **Jesus Christ had to be born in order to be raised from the dead.** The law of death had to be reversed.

- Finally, to prove the fact of reconciliation of man with God and His favor toward the former, the Lord had to take up a man into His holy presence. That was the very reason the **Messiah was born — to be taken up to the heavens.**

The essence of these strategic tasks of salvation is what determines the titles of the following chapters of this book. I hope with all my heart that after reading it you will see in an entirely different light the abundance of riches stored up for you personally in the facts that Christ was…

>Born to die.
>>Born to live.
>>>Born to be raised from the dead.
>>>>Born to save.
>>>>>Born to ascend to the heavens.

CHAPTER I
THE MYSTERY OF DIVINE INCARNATION

If then David calls him Lord,
how is he his son?" | Matt. 22:45

As was already mentioned, the task of the church on earth is, first of all, to establish and exalt God's truth, or, as Paul puts it, to be its "pillar" — a display of sorts. The church does not handle trivial matters that could be taken lightly and irresponsibly. The truth entrusted to her care speaks of God's greatness and, therefore, may not be preached without trembling.

It is like your car breaking down. And to try to help you out, a friend allows you to use his 20-year-old Chevy Cavalier. Of course, you would be grateful for any help and would get behind the wheel of this clunker. But imagine that the CEO of the large corporation where your friend works finds out about your misfortune and offers you his new SUV. You would, without doubt, accept this offer ecstatically, but you would also treat the car with much greater care!

The same is true for the world of ideas and values: The more influential their author, the less likely we are to treat them casually and the more natural our own acceptance of these principles.

The mystery of godliness described by Paul is basically rooted in Who our Lord Jesus Christ is and what part He plays in the universe.

> If I delay, you may know how one ought to behave in the household of God, which is the church of the living God, a pillar and buttress of the truth. Great indeed, we confess, is the mystery of godliness: **He was manifested in the flesh, vindicated by the Spirit, seen by angels, proclaimed among the nations, believed on in the world, taken up in glory.** (1 Tim. 3:15–16)

Salvation of humanity was an extremely difficult task. In the eyes of the devil and his demons, it looked absolutely undoable. Even the hosts of heaven's angels were astonished at the wisdom and the unexpected nature of God's solution. Recall the angels' song over the fields of Bethlehem! Christ's incarnation introduced an element into the spiritual frame of reference that was previously unknown in the universe — a God-Man! But not everyone was in a hurry to admit it.

Let us for a few minutes leave the triumphant heavens and stupefied hell and push our way through the throng of those who beheld the Son of God with their own eyes. Let us listen to those whose company, even back then, was almost entirely off limits to regular folks. Let us look at the mortals, shouting out their questions to God.

| THE PARADOX OF GOD INCARNATE |

There was a day when literally all of the Jewish religious ruling classes were gathered in one place: Herodians and Sadducees, Pharisees and scribes. One common goal unified this motley crowd: the fight against the Teacher Who was gaining popularity with the people. Everyone hoped to corner Him with a question. Every attempt touched upon burning social issues: *Is it okay to pay taxes to our oppressors? Do people get married in eternity? Which commandment is the most important?*

Today, we know the answers to these questions. But let's imagine that day and time. Christ's disciples must have felt like a frog on a hot skillet. But Jesus countered every attack brilliantly. Moreover, in addition to giving no one an opportunity to accuse Him, He also provided in His answers crucially important lessons on the Kingdom of God.

Then finally, Jesus addressed His opponents, who found themselves out of arguments. He spoke with complete calm. His question back to them was not a tricky one. Not a trace of bitterness or vengeance. No arrogance. In spite of the thinly veiled hostility these people breathed toward Him, Jesus Christ seemed magnanimously unfrazzled by it. His question was an attempt to unlock their consciousness so that they could grasp the problem underlying their attacks. It was not His goal to corner them like they tried to corner Him. Neither did He want to damage their prestige. He sincerely meant to help them think...

> Now while the Pharisees were gathered together, Jesus asked them a question, saying:
>
> "What do you think about the Christ? Whose son is he?"
>
> They said to him, "The son of David."
>
> He said to them, "How is it then that David, in the Spirit, calls him Lord, saying, "'The Lord said to my Lord, "Sit at my right hand, until I put your enemies under your feet"'? If then David calls him Lord, how is he his son?"
>
> And no one was able to answer him a word, nor from that day did anyone dare to ask him any more questions. (Matt. 22:41–46).

With His question Jesus prompted the religious leaders to take a closer look at what the Scriptures said about the Messiah.

That was a very serious issue, one of vital importance for Pharisees in general, and in that situation in particular. Why? Because they were face to face with the Messiah — and they failed to recognize Him! It was for this purpose that Jesus quoted to them this text from the book of Psalms, clearly indicating that Messiah must be God.

The problem Jewish leaders had was that they missed the very essence of the religion they so zealously pursued: the worship of the true God.

These brilliant people painstakingly studied religious Law. They made sure all the rules and rites were observed in a precise and timely manner. Their entire life revolved around it. They were sacrificial, having completely dedicated themselves to God.

But in the process, unnoticed by those around them and by themselves, the Pharisees created a religion of their own. This religion preserved many of the external attributes of the Jewish faith. Yet their godliness was devoid of life. By focusing entirely on the rules, they forgot the Lawgiver. Burning with the desire to comprehend and keep the Law, they were rendered absolutely incapable of discerning its Author.

Today, just like then, there are many Christians who resemble Pharisees so much that it is appalling. They read and study the Holy Scriptures for hours, perhaps adding the learning of ancient languages, culture, and history. They dedicate themselves to reflection and disputes on secondary theological topics so much that they begin to see those things as the main tenets of Christianity. They give large sums of money to advance church activities. They sacrifice time to serve others. They dedicate all they are and all they have — all the while forgetting about the Life. They forget the One Whom they should be worshipping.

These modern Pharisees reduce their Christianity to simple rule following. When they hear of worshipping God and having a relationship with Him, they blurt out impatiently, "All right, all right, we get all that. Now, tell us what we need to do."

In reality, an understanding of how to act properly is only possible when we know God personally, when we have a deep, consistent relationship with Him, when we practice actual living worship.

This is why Jesus Christ asks the Pharisees a simple question: Who is the Messiah? This is like a clue, given by the professor at an exam. They are on the verge of failing this test. They are about to give the Son of God to be crucified. So, He reminds them: Think again, who is Christ? Who is He supposed to be?

> Jesus asked them a question, saying: "What do you think about the Christ? Whose son is he?"
>
> They said to him, "The son of David."

Instead of pausing and thinking, the Pharisees blurt out a standard answer which was technically correct. The Messiah did actually have to be a son of David. However, Jesus Christ wants to show them an entirely different aspect of this issue. The Messiah, while being the Son of David, while being a man, is at the same time God. And the Holy Scriptures speak clearly of this.

> He said to them, "How is it then that David, in the Spirit, calls him Lord, saying, 'The Lord said to my Lord, "Sit at my right hand, until I put your enemies under your feet"'?
>
> If then David calls him Lord, how is he his son?"

But, you see, this file is nowhere to be found in the Pharisees' database! They know that the Messiah is the Son of David. Yet, all the texts that talk about the Messiah's divine nature don't seem to exist to them. And there is a reason why: pride!

Christ's opponents approached the Law as expert researchers and not as sinners in need of salvation. Their knowledge and success in following the commandments were not inspired by being humble before God, but rather by a desire to outdo others' performance. As a result, their religion became encumbered with a slew of human rules, scholastic rhetoric and ceremonialism. Instead of bringing them closer to God, it began alienating them from Him.

They began treating God and His Word as if they knew and understood it all. Scriptural passages representing God in all His majesty ceased to inspire awe and trembling in them. And a terrible thing happened to these religious people: They created an image of the Messiah based on their own ideas.

Instead of acknowledging the tension between the passages talking of Christ-Man and Christ-God, they pushed the idea of the Messiah's deity into the shadows and chose to see Him only as the Son of David — as a Superhuman Who was supposed to restore the kingdom of Israel and ensure a carefree future for the Jews. The idea of divine incarnation proved to be too difficult for them to grasp. It betrayed the weakness of their minds, and as such it was rejected.

By misusing Scripture to support the god they created, they fell prey to the greatest delusion, which ultimately led to the crucifixion of the unrecognized Son of God.

With His question Jesus Christ directly confronted this problem and revealed that the biblical teaching on the Messiah was much more complex that it might have seemed to the Jewish rulers. Jesus exposed the insufficiency of human logic — man's attempt to determine the proper place for each piece of the puzzle in the divine panorama of history. God's wisdom superseded the abilities of the scribes and the Pharisees to comprehend it. And Christ wanted to help them to see this great God.

One of our biggest problems is that we try to measure everything in life by our own standards and abilities. We discard everything that does not fit in this box.

Have you ever tried thinking what is beyond the last star? Give it a try! Just lean back in your chair and try imagining infinity… It will not take long for your mind to begin to explode. We as mankind are limited. We cannot grasp the concept of infinity.

It troubles us to think of the limitless expanse of space. We find it problematic to take in how everything came out of nothing. That is why people came up with the theory of evolution, the Big Bang theory, and others like them. They want to find a construct that would help fit this big, complex world into their small, primitive minds. Why? Because they find it hard to believe that God spoke and that out of the void, out of a vacuum, came matter — and not just matter, but matter in its most complex forms, harmoniously maintained by a myriad of laws.

God created the universe in such a way that people would tremble just looking at it — so that they could see clearly that they do not have the world under control, and so that, no manner how many millennia they could spend on this earth, they would never cease to discover new mysteries revealing the incredible intelligence of the Creator.

This is the very reason we remember Christmas. It is not just about some good songs. It is not just about decorations on Christmas trees. Even though this is all beautiful and speaks of purity, kindness, and the warmth of a home, it is not the point. When we approach Christmas, we come face to face with the incomprehensible phenomenon of the Messiah incarnate.

It is impossible to fit Him into the framework of human existence. The limitless God entered the limits of our material world and became a real Man. It is infinitely difficult for us to comprehend how God the Creator could assume the limitations of creation. We are unable to embrace mentally all of the implications of this phenomenon, and therefore we often choose to skip over it.

When asking this question of the Pharisees, Jesus draws the attention of everyone reading the Bible to something that religion often misses: the necessity of serious and profound reflection on His greatness and inconceivability.

The realization of the mystery of Christ's simultaneously divine and human nature is a source of life-giving strength to every believer. Without it, faith is reduced to a dead religion. And from there, crucifixion is but a few steps away....

GOD RECOGNIZED ON YOUR KNEES

People tend to simplify everything that goes beyond their comprehension. For instance, the Scriptures teach that God is entirely sovereign in directing people's destinies, yet every one of us is entirely liable for our actions. People have a hard time reconciling these two statements and the seeming conflict between them. That is why they try to reduce such doctrines to the level of their intellectual capacities: either God is not sovereign, or humans cannot be held liable. But under either of these theories, the limited human mind rejects divine revelation. This renders religion weak, causes worship without confidence, and leaves life plain and ineffective.

It is so much easier to do something for God than to get to know Him the way He is. When we think of God, it is so much easier to see rules, commandments, and ceremonies than to attempt to comprehend His incomprehensible nature. It is so much easier to reduce life to what a praying Pharisee summed up this way: "I fast twice a week, I tithe, I do not commit outrageous sins, unlike others..." He came, rattled off his report, and off he went! Simple formulas, perhaps very good formulas indeed.

Yet, in the Holy Scriptures we see how systematically, from one passage to another, God reveals Himself as incomprehensible. Introducing us to the story of the life of Christ, the Holy Spirit puts us face to face with this God-Man — on the one hand, quite simple and approachable, and on the other, mysterious, extraordinary and amazing.

This obvious contradiction is given to us, and not for the purpose of resolving it. It is there to instill in us a trembling before God and a humble trust in Him. Instead of reducing God to simplified formulas, we must come in contact with the divine traits of the Person of Christ so that we can actually live through Him.

We need to ponder, admire, and pursue with our minds the Person of the Savior, which is so much greater than us. Jehovah revealed His greatness to us in Jesus in the most possibly intimate way. And we should treasure this amazing experience! It will ever astonish us. It will always humble and overwhelm us, but at the same time, it will give us a firm foundation in life.

God wants us to practice this worship in spite of the inconceivability of divine incarnation. Or rather, God wants us to realize and gaze upon Him for the very reason that divine incarnation is inconceivable!

THE DEPTHS OF THE RICHES

We need to seek the Lord. We need not only to seek out in the Bible information about what we should do. We need to constantly grow in the realization of Who God is. But every real contact with God will inevitably put us face to face with His inconceivability.

In the oldest book of the Bible, the book of Job, Elihu, one of the friends of the sufferer, said this:

> Behold, God is great, and we know him not; the number of his years is unsearchable. (Job 36:26)

It has always been this way. Whenever God would reveal Himself to a human, it was always followed by a manifestation of His astonishing greatness.

When the people of Israel came in direct contact with Jehovah at the foot of Mount Sinai, the Lord's presence overwhelmed and shook them:

The Mystery of Divine Incarnation | 35

> Now when all the people saw the thunder and the flashes of lightning and the sound of the trumpet and the mountain smoking, the people were afraid and trembled, and they stood far off and said to Moses, "You speak to us, and we will listen; but do not let God speak to us, lest we die." (Exod. 20:18–19)

This is something we need, friends. Instead of endeavoring to accomplish great things for God, all we need is to simply stand before Him. His greatness will overwhelm our hearts to the core, turning upside down our religion of works and transforming every step we take into an act of worship.

Answering the frightened Jews, Moses explained that a real encounter with God is of crucial importance for man to learn the fear of the Lord:

> Moses said to the people, "Do not fear, for God has come to test you, that the fear of him may be before you, that you may not sin." (Exod. 20:20)

If we do not behold God, if we do not practice standing before Him, we soon forget Whom we walk before, and then religion is quickly reduced to rules, rituals, and arguments as to who understands better the nuances of the Law, who keeps the commandments, and who does not. The fear of the Lord — that is the true source of obedience, and it is only developed in the presence of God, the way it happened to prophet Isaiah:

> In the year that King Uzziah died I saw the Lord sitting upon a throne, high and lifted up; and the train of his robe filled the temple.
>
> Above him stood the seraphim. Each had six wings: with two he covered his face, and with two he covered his feet, and with two he flew. And one called to another and said:
>
> "Holy, holy, holy is the Lord of hosts; the whole earth is full of his glory!"
>
> And the foundations of the thresholds shook at the voice of him who called, and the house was filled with smoke. And I said:
>
> **"Woe is me! For I am lost; for I am a man of unclean lips, and I dwell in the midst of a people of unclean lips;** for my eyes have seen the King, the Lord of hosts!" (Isa. 6:1–5)

This man saw himself in the light of the Holy God — and he trembled!

Every time I come across theologians and religious leaders speculating on various arguments concerning the Lord, I have a feeling that they may have never, or at most may have very rarely, encountered the true, real God, and that they likely have a very limited experience of practical time spent before the Almighty. To them, the incomprehensible God remains an object of laboratory research, disputes, futile religious activities — anything but the One Who defeats their logic and crushes their hearts.

The apostle Paul, when encountering manifestations of divine wisdom, simply began to write poetry. His letters periodically feature such poetic outbursts. One of them is the eleventh chapter of the epistle to the Romans.

He just finished presenting the Gospel, just finished explaining the key points of salvation. And here is his response to the realization of the unique plan of God:

> Oh, the depth of the riches and wisdom and knowledge of God! How unsearchable are his judgments and how inscrutable his ways!
>
> "For who has known the mind of the Lord, or who has been his counselor?" "Or who has given a gift to him that he might be repaid?"
>
> For from him and through him and to him are all things. To him be glory forever. Amen. (Rom. 11:33−36)

True intimacy with God causes awe! This is one of the main reasons why we need to seek God. Encountering His inconceivability teaches us a right attitude toward God Himself.

BLESSED ARE THE "FOOLS"

Divine incarnation was the most vibrant revelation of God to mankind. If people experienced sacred trembling due to God's *invisible* presence, His *visible* expression of Himself should have had an even greater effect.

When we talk about Jesus Christ, we are not merely dealing with a historical personality. Neither are we dealing with just a prophet who showed signs and worked miracles. We are dealing with God Himself! While it is absolutely impossible for us to have a full understanding of the Lord, it is even more difficult to grasp how God became man. The Scriptures tells it to us in these terms:

Long ago, at many times and in many ways, God spoke to our fathers by the prophets, but in these last days he has spoken to us by his Son, whom he appointed the heir of all things, through whom also he created the world.

> **He is the radiance of the glory of God and the exact imprint of his nature, and he upholds the universe by the word of his power.** After making purification for sins, he sat down at the right hand of the Majesty on high. (Heb. 1:1–3)

This passage presents Jesus Christ as the "radiance of the glory" of God the Father.

The Messiah came to earth, assuming human flesh. However, this taking on of flesh did not limit nor diminish His ability to radiate God's intrinsic glory.

Christ is called here "the exact imprint of [God's] nature," or an exact reflection of the Father — which means that we may make inferences concerning the character and intentions of the Father from what we've seen in the Son. And this is what is so amazing: Christ introduced the unapproachable God to the world of men!

Another attribute emphasized here is the power of the God Almighty which the Son of God possessed. Even with lack of sleep, exhaustion, and hunger, He was still the One Whose word maintained the whole world. In this brief description, the author points to Christ and exclaims, "Look Who is here! It is the Father Himself!"

Christ stunned people with His inconceivability. At the beginning, Mary and Joseph were astonished by the miracle of this Baby's immaculate conception. When Mary heard what kind of mission God had chosen for her, she had a very legitimate question: "How will this be?"

If you notice, the Angel's answer does little to explain how this would happen: "The Holy Spirit will come upon you, and the power of the Most High will overshadow you; therefore the child to be born will be called holy — the Son of God" (Luke 1:35). This was all he said because the miracle of divine incarnation is impossible to explain. The human mind is incapable of comprehending it. This goes beyond physiology, beyond our understanding of the structure of the cell. But, friends, we're dealing with the One Who invented the cell. We're dealing with the Author of physiology, with the One Who created a physical body out of nothing!

Christ amazed old Simeon as well with His divine humanity when the latter held God in his hands and realized, "This child is appointed for the fall and rising of many in Israel" (Luke 2:34).

Later, He astounded John the Baptist, who said,

> Behold, the Lamb of God, who takes away the sin of the world! This is he of whom I said, 'After me comes a man who ranks before me, because he was before me.' (John 1:29–30).

Try to make sense of what John is saying: "After me comes a man," "he was before me," "ranks before me." Judging from John's questions that follow, the prophet himself does not even fully comprehend the scale of what is taking place. But he is voicing what God is revealing to him at this moment. And he realizes that standing before him is the Lamb…the eternal One Who was there before him. And he is deeply shaken.

He also astonished His disciples who said in amazement, "Who then is this, that even the wind and the sea obey him?" (Mark 4:41). They saw in Jesus the Messiah the incomprehensible God-Man living out a real human life right before their eyes.

Did they have all the answers about Christ? No. Did they understand how the immaculate conception happened? Absolutely not! Were they able to explain how divinity was combined with humanity? They couldn't. But they knew for certain that they saw God before them. That was a fact. In spite of times of weakness and despair, when asked, "Who do people say that the Son of Man is?" (Matt. 6:13), they answered without hesitation,

> You are the Christ, the Son of the living God. (Matt. 16:16)

And when Christ asked them, "Do you want to go away as well?" after a large group of His followers left Him, Peter voiced the opinion shared by the twelve:

> Lord, to whom shall we go? You have the words of eternal life, and we have believed, and have come to know, that you are the Holy One of God. (John 6:68–69)

And Jesus asked the same question of the scribes and the Pharisees — a question everyone must answer: *Who is Christ?*

The Pharisees' problem was that, though they had the same information available to them as Mary, Simeon, John, and Peter — who all saw God in Christ — these connoisseurs of the Bible couldn't reconcile in their minds the concept of divine incarnation and simply rejected it outright.

What do *you* think of Christ?

To the Pharisees, He was just the son of David, which meant he had to be subject to their system and live by their rules — something He could not do....This was their great tragedy. And one day, Jesus told them plainly what prevented them from seeing Him as the Messiah: it was their unwillingness to bow down to God and His authority.

> So the Jews gathered around him and said to him, "How long will you keep us in suspense? If you are the Christ, tell us plainly."
>
> Jesus answered them, "I told you, and you do not believe. The works that I do in my Father's name bear witness about me, but you do not believe because you are not among my sheep. My sheep hear my voice, and I know them, and they follow me. (John 10:24–27)

Look at this picture: Many have already confessed that Jesus is the Christ, the Son of God, yet these religious experts still do not get it! They come to Him and say, "Give us more miracles! Show us again. Convince us!"

Wait, do His sheep understand everything? Do believers know what God is "made of," so to speak? No. But the sheep know the Shepherd's voice and follow Him in obedience. God's children do not claim to understand everything. When faced with the inconceivability of God's nature, they can't explain how Christ combined humanity and divinity, how God could cry or allow men to crucify Him, or ultimately — how God could die.

These and other difficult questions do not leave true sheep confused. On the contrary, the mystery of Jesus Christ convinces them of His otherworldly origin. It emphasizes the greatness of the Son of God. It leads believers to even greater humility before Him. It encourages the fear of the Lord and trust in Him.

As for those who have no faith, who haven't bowed down to God with heartbreak over their sin, to them the truth of the divine incarnation — and of salvation in general — seems absurd. The apostle Paul once said this plainly:

> For since, in the wisdom of God, the world did not know God through wisdom, it pleased God through the folly of what we preach to save those who believe.
>
> For Jews demand signs and Greeks seek wisdom, but we preach Christ crucified, a stumbling block to Jews and folly to Gentiles, but to those who are called, both Jews and Greeks, Christ the power of God and the wisdom of God.
>
> For **the foolishness of God is wiser than men**, and the weakness of God is stronger than men. (1 Cor. 1:21-25)

| THE GOD-MAN |

Christ's divine humanity has caused arguments throughout history. When people are faced with the inconceivable nature of this phenomenon, they usually respond in one of two incorrect ways: They either end up confused, or (like the Pharisees) they try to hush this fact down.

The fear of looking foolish may tempt us as well to simplify the Gospel and throw the baby out with the bathwater. Faulty approaches to this issue have already served as the basis for many false doctrines. If you study the first ecumenical councils, you will discover that they all convened to resolve issues dealing directly or indirectly with Christ's nature.

The first false doctrine was *Gnosticism*. Gnostics denied the humanity of Christ. They claimed that the flesh, like the rest of the physical world, is the epitome of evil. Since Jesus Christ was God and goodness incarnate, He could not have been in the flesh, and therefore His supposedly physical flesh was only a semblance, an optical illusion of sorts.

No ecumenical council was ever called to discuss the ideas of Gnosticism because the apostles — contemporaries of the Gnostics — spoke very plainly against this heresy in their writings in the Scripture.

On the other hand, *Arians* denied Christ's divine nature and taught that He was merely the highest of all creation. This false doctrine managed to exist for quite a long time. For a short period, Arianism was even adopted as the orthodox position of the Christian church.

Nestorians believed the deception that Christ was born as an ordinary man, and that only when He became a mature man did God fill Him up morally and dwell in Him as in a temple. They could not comprehend how God could humble Himself to come as an infant.

Monophysites taught that in Christ humanity was completely assimilated in the divine. In other words, there was humanity in Christ, but the divine dominated it completely and "pushed the human under." As a result, the human side of Christ was virtually inactive.

Monothelites, while acknowledging both natures, denied that Christ exhibited a human will. In their opinion, Christ was God-Man, and His desires were God's desires only. His human will was in a state of atrophy.

Disputes concerning the divine-and-human nature of Christ at the ecumenical level only died down at the sixth council in 680 AD. The representatives of churches in attendance at that council completely rejected the doctrine of the Monothelites, affirming that Christ's human will was absolutely real yet in complete obedience to divine will.

Notice the great number of opinions! And all this for one reason: people cannot handle the mental pressure of God's unfathomable ways!

False doctrines, arising out of a misunderstanding of Christ's nature, exist in our day, too. The most well-known sect that continues playing games with Christ's divine-and-human nature is the Jehovah's Witnesses. They cannot grasp how Jesus Christ was God and man at the same time. They believe Him to be a great prophet, nothing more. The Mormons have a similar problem with more radical differences.

All of these alternatives are proof that the issue of Christ's divine-and-human nature is beyond our intellectual capacities. But friends, the Scripture never, in any passage, gives us reason to believe that God is our equal, that we can easily understand His ways, that we can effortlessly solve the mysteries of His great plans for the universe.

The God of the Bible is always the same: inconceivable, astonishing, inspiring fear by His holiness.

The Bible does not even attempt to explain to us that which is beyond our comprehension. The only thing the Bible tells us is, "Believe!" And it is not because faith has some mystical function. Due to the limitations of our minds, we can comprehend only up to a certain point, and then we must employ faith.

Even the development of the sciences has not happened within one generation. Humans did not make a quick leap from observing a bird's flight to building a spaceship. We accumulate collective experiences in order to move from one level of knowledge to the next, because the amount of information that exists in the world surpasses the mental abilities of any one person.

God — He Who possesses all knowledge and Who was its author — is infinitely more complex than any science. His person and being are beyond our ability to comprehend. We constantly face a myriad of facts testifying to His existence, His character, and His works, yet due to our limited minds, we cannot see the depth of His nature and His Person. All that is left is to believe, trusting in the authority of God's revelation.

Having faith does not make us special. Faith merely simplifies our life. If we devoted our lives to understanding fully how God works, it would drive us crazy. The mental pressure is simply too much. It is beyond the limitations of our minds. That is why we accept by faith the realities God explains to us in His Word. And that is why the Scripture, when talking about Jesus Christ as both God and man, simply states what He is without attempting to prove it.

> For now we see in a mirror dimly, but then face to face. Now I know in part; then I shall know fully, even as I have been fully known. (1 Cor. 13:12)

The Scripture is unashamed in this regard. Just like it does not try to prove God exists, just like it does not explain how God created the physical world, in the same way the Bible does not present any defense of divine humanity.

It gives a definitive description of Christ as God and man, without responding to the tension between various passages and without the slightest attempt at explaining how to tie them together. It gives us an opportunity to know the truth and believe in it so that we can live and function in this universe, built by God in such a sophisticated and complex way.

PROOF OF CHRIST'S HUMANITY

So, let's set history aside and open the Bible to see what the Scriptures say, first, about Christ's humanity.

Promised as a man

We see it from the very first pages of the Bible. While pronouncing judgment on the serpent who had seduced

Eve, God introduces the Messiah for the first time and presents Him precisely as the seed of the woman:

> I will put enmity between you and the woman,
>   and between your offspring and her offspring;
> he shall bruise your head,
>   and you shall bruise his heel. (Gen. 3:15)

When the Pharisees were asked whose Son the Messiah should be, they answered without thinking, "The son of David" (Matt. 22:42). The apostle Matthew presents Christ with the same description at the beginning of his Gospel:

> The book of the genealogy of Jesus Christ, the son of David, the son of Abraham. (Matt. 1:1)

The Jews, without a doubt, realized that the Messiah had to be an *extraordinary* man, but no one had any doubt that it would be a *man*.

Born as a man

> And while they were there, the time came for her to give birth. And she gave birth to her firstborn son and wrapped him in swaddling cloths and laid him in a manger, because there was no place for them in the inn. (Luke 2:6–7)

It is said of Christ that He was born as a man. Look at the completely natural picture described here: "she gave birth," "wrapped him in swaddling cloths," "laid him in a manger." These are the realities of a human birth.

But often these statements cause people to question how it was possible for God to be a helpless baby depending on earthly parents? It is one thing to accept Jesus as a man who came in full power, but when He is incapable of caring for Himself, when this Baby needed his clothes changed, when He needed to be fed on time — how was that possible?

And have you ever wondered how the God-Man's human development — how His intellect and worldview were "formed"? Did He need to get to know the world? How did He "learn" to talk? It is virtually impossible to comprehend these things about Christ. Yet the Scripture simply informs us of the fact of His very human life, foregoing any detailed explanations.

Having lived as a man

Christ liked referring to Himself as the "Son of Man." He emphasized it constantly. Here is one example:

> And Jesus said to him, "Foxes have holes, and birds of the air have nests, but the Son of Man has nowhere to lay his head." (Matt. 8:20)

Christ was no stranger to our daily routine. The Son of Man did need a roof over His head and food for sustenance. He needed to rest just like we do. He was not a "man of steel."

Christ also developed and maintained social ties. He had family, friends, neighbors. He was invited to weddings, and not only in His hometown. People knew Him very well, as well as his parents, brothers, sisters — He was *their* carpenter from Nazareth.

He communicated with these people just like we communicate with each other. But we are shocked by the thought that God could meet someone on the way home from work, pat them on the back, admit how tired He was from the day spent at the shop, and ask them about their family and affairs. And then that same man could go home, kneel down, and tell all this to God all over again....

Jesus worked, and He knew how exhausting physical labor is. Christ had a creative side to Him. Carpentry is a fine and intricate craft. The Scripture also mentions that Christ often suffered hunger and thirst. Like everyone else, He felt like sleeping a few extra minutes in the morning.

Jesus was not a "hothouse plant" and did not live the life of a spoiled, royal child. He experienced problems as we do. If you, sitting by the fire among Christ's disciples, had talked to Him of the hardships of life, He could have said with sincere empathy, "I know how you feel!"

Died as a man

During His life here on earth, the Messiah was not immune to suffering, disease, injury, or even death. He did not survive on earth with a huge dose of pain killers. He lived just like an ordinary man: He experienced real pain.

> [Jesus Christ], though he was in the form of God, did not count equality with God a thing to be grasped, but emptied himself, by taking the form of a servant, being born in the likeness of men. And being found in human form, he humbled himself by becoming obedient to the point of death, even death on a cross. (Phil. 2:6−8)

The Scripture portrays Jesus Christ as an actual man who had the worst of life experiences. Here are words spoken by Jesus Himself:

> See, we are going up to Jerusalem. And **the Son of Man** will be delivered over to the chief priests and scribes, and they will condemn him to death and deliver him over to the Gentiles to be mocked and flogged and crucified, and he will be raised on the third day. (Matt. 20:18-19)

Chapter 22 of the Gospel of Luke depicts for us Jesus Christ's agony prior to His arrest:

> And he withdrew from them about a stone's throw, and knelt down and prayed, saying, "Father, if you are willing, remove this cup from me. Nevertheless, not my will, but yours, be done."
>
> And there appeared to him an angel from heaven, strengthening him. And being in agony he prayed more earnestly; and his sweat became like great drops of blood falling down to the ground. (Luke 22:41−44)

This speaks of the huge physical pressure Christ felt. This presents Him as a real, living human being — with a body and nerves. He was a human that felt at that moment the overbearing burden of human sin.

Beside the physical effects, Jesus suffered spiritually. He had no comfort. He was in agony. He was struggling against the flesh. It was an unbearable internal battle.

Have you experienced sleepless nights before something difficult? Have you worried about something so much that you've spend the whole day thinking about only that? Have you had to wrestle with your own will knowing you would go through pain and humiliation?

What Christ had to go through was many times worse than anything we have known. He came to His disciples, only to find them sleeping when sleep was the last thing on His mind. He would have loved to zone out and forget about the approaching crowd and soldiers, but such was His reality. In the final moments prior to being betrayed, He is imploring His Father for the cup of suffering to be removed from Him, and we can only imagine how excruciating it must have been for Him to say, "Nevertheless, not my will, but yours, be done"!

As he died, he was a man. He experienced the entire range of physical and emotional suffering.

Taken up to heaven as a man

Speaking about His second coming, Jesus emphasized that He would be known in heaven as the Son of Man:

> For **the Son of Man** is going to come with his angels in the glory of his Father, and then he will repay each person according to what he has done. (Matt. 16:27)

In another passage Paul unequivocally talks about the eternal significance of Jesus Christ as a man:

> For there is one God, and there is one mediator between God and men, **the man Christ Jesus**, who gave himself as a ransom for all, which is the testimony given at the proper time. (1 Tim. 2:5−6)

In order to become the Redeemer and Intercessor for mankind, Christ had to become human. We will later expand on the reason why it had to be so. But it remains a fact we cannot ignore.

So, we see that the Holy Scriptures emphatically and unambiguously present the Messiah as a man.

PROOF OF JESUS' DIVINITY

Promised as God

When asking the Pharisees about the Messiah's nature, Jesus quoted a prophecy given by David and recorded in Psalm 110:

> The Lord says to my Lord: "Sit at my right hand, until I make your enemies your footstool." (Ps. 110:1)

In this passage David spoke about his offspring and an heir to his throne. Yet, instead of emphasizing his superiority over him, the king placed himself in a position of submission. In this verse David used the words "Yahweh" and "Adonai," in a place of the word "Lord". Both words traditionally describe the God of Israel. When we see the phrase: "The Lord says to my Lord," we should read it as, "Yahweh says to Adonai, 'Sit at my right hand.'"

Recalling this passage, Jesus Christ emphasized that David himself spoke about Him, the Messiah, as Lord, using the name God had called Himself throughout all of the Old Testament. So, He was not merely a man.

The Jews were very familiar with this passage. The only problem was that they did not want to interpret it literally. Every time it was discussed they preferred to avoid the subject.

Yet it was not just David — other Old Testament prophets also foretold that the Messiah would be God incarnate. One of the most explicit examples is found in the Book of Isaiah:

> For to us **a child is born**,
>   to us a son is given;
> and the government shall be upon his shoulder,
>   and his name shall be called
> Wonderful Counselor, **Mighty God**,
>   **Everlasting Father, Prince of Peace.** (Isa. 9:6)

This passage directly calls the Messiah God leaving us no alternative interpretation. It is crystal clear: Mighty God, Everlasting Father, Prince of Peace. The verses focus our attention on several characteristics at once that are exclusive attributes of a divine person.

The Old Testament has no shortage of references to the Messiah as God.

Acting as God

In various situations throughout Christ's earthly ministry many people realized clearly that they were dealing with God. When Peter, in obedience to Jesus, caught a huge amount of fish against all natural laws, he knew — Jesus was not a simple prophet.

> When Simon Peter saw it, he fell down at Jesus' knees, saying, **"Depart from me, for I am a sinful man, O Lord."** For he and all who were with him were astonished at the catch of fish that they had taken. (Luke 5:8–9)

Peter was a professional fisherman. Where, when, and how to fish was something for a fisherman, not a carpenter, to decide. However, when Peter found himself face to face with a manifestation of the supernatural power and knowledge of the Son of God, he dropped to the bottom of the boat, afraid to even look at Him. All of a sudden, he realized in Whose presence he was standing. This is why he started begging, "Please, leave me. I am unclean. You are too holy for me to be in Your presence." Suddenly, he saw clearly that the true God was before him — and he was filled with horror! Now, that is a genuine encounter with God, my friends!

The Gospel of Mark describes another situation that shook the disciples to their core.

> And he awoke and rebuked the wind and said to the sea, "Peace! Be still!" And the wind ceased, and there was a great calm…. And they were filled with great fear and said to one another, "Who then is this, that even the wind and the sea obey him?" (Mark 4:39, 41)

Miracles, wonders, healings, casting out of demons, teaching with authority — all this was so obvious that even Jewish rulers realized deep in their hearts that they were dealing with Someone Who came from God.

> This man [Nicodemus] came to Jesus by night and said to him, "Rabbi, we know that you are a teacher come from God, for no one can do these signs that you do unless God is with him." (John 3:2)

Presented as God

Jesus Christ Himself spoke unequivocally of the fact that He was God. For example, when Jesus responded to Peter's famous statement, He did not forbid him from calling Him God. He affirmed a disciple.

> Simon Peter replied, "You are the Christ, the Son of the living God."
>
> And Jesus answered him, "Blessed are you, Simon Bar-Jonah! For flesh and blood has not revealed this to you, but my Father who is in heaven. (Matt. 16:16–17)

Even though some liberal theologians today try to interpret Jesus' words in a way that excludes any claim to divinity in them, the people these words were originally addressed to interpreted them only one way: they realized that Christ was calling Himself God.

When Jews approached Christ for the umpteenth time, demanding a miracle that would prove He was the Messiah, Jesus explained that there had already been enough proof shown, and he concluded His speech with a declaration:

> "I and the Father are one."
>
> The Jews picked up stones again to stone him.
>
> Jesus answered them, "I have shown you many good works from the Father; for which of them are you going to stone me?"
>
> The Jews answered him, "It is not for a good work that we are going to stone you but for blasphemy, because you, being a man, make yourself God." (John 10:30–33)

There was no ambiguity for the Jews in Jesus' words. He referred to Himself as God, and that was the very reason they grabbed rocks to stone Him. This was the way to punish blasphemers, and they believed Jesus to be one of them.

We find a number of similar situations in Scripture. For example, at one point, when the Jews heard Jesus promise that someone who keeps His word will never see death, they were instantly offended:

> "Are you greater than our father Abraham, who died? And the prophets died! Who do you make yourself out to be?"
>
> Jesus answered, "If I glorify myself, my glory is nothing. It is my Father who glorifies me, of whom you say, 'He is our God.' But you have not known him. I know him. If I were to say that I do not know him, I would be a liar like you, but I do know him and I keep his word.
>
> Your father Abraham rejoiced that he would see my day. He saw it and was glad."
>
> So the Jews said to him, "You are not yet fifty years old, and have you seen Abraham?" (John 8:53–57)

The following phrase is the clearest statement of Christ's divinity in His own words:

> Jesus said to them, "Truly, truly, I say to you, before Abraham was, **I am**." So they picked up stones to throw at him, but Jesus hid himself and went out of the temple. (John 8:58–59)

You know what enraged the Jews? Two words: "I am."

Just look for yourselves how this simple clause is built. When talking about Abraham, Jesus uses the past tense of the verb "to be" — *Abraham was*. Yet when referring to Himself, He uses the same verb, but in the present tense, thus emphasizing His eternal nature: "Before Abraham was, *I am*" — which means, "I always was."

However, the strong effect of this statement was due to the fact that Jesus said these words in Aramaic, which is very closely related to Ancient Hebrew. If one reads this passage in the original, he cannot help but be astonished at the realization of *what* it is Christ says: The literal translation of the words "I am" is "Yahweh" — God's sacred Name. *That* is why the Jews reached for the rocks again.

It was unheard of for someone to be stoned right in the temple. But Christ's declaration of His divine nature enraged His listeners to the core. They were ready to kill Him right there, even in the holy place.

In summary, Jesus said He was God. The prophets said He was God. He acted as God. But, more importantly, the Father, together with the Holy Spirit, testified of Him as God.

Judge for yourselves: Who could claim to be God — while not being God — and remain alive? Wasn't this what Gamaliel said?

> So in the present case I tell you, keep away from these men and let them alone, for if this plan or this undertaking is of man, it will fail; but if it is of God, you will not be able to overthrow them. You might even be found opposing God!" (Acts 5:38–39)

In addition to the prophetic declaration David made in Psalm 110, God publicly testified at least three times to Christ's divinity: at Jesus' baptism, at His transfiguration, and at the moment of Christ's entry into Jerusalem. Every time God's words were approximately the same:

> And a voice came out of the cloud, saying, "This is my Son, my Chosen One; listen to him!" (Luke 9:35)

And finally, the truth of these words is also confirmed by the third Person of the divine Trinity, the Holy Spirit.

> Who is it that overcomes the world except the one who believes that Jesus is the Son of God? This is he who came by water and blood — Jesus Christ; not by the water only but by the water and the blood. **And the Spirit is the one who testifies**, because the Spirit is the truth. (1 John 5:5–6)

| THE IMPORTANCE OF THE TRUTH OF GOD IN THE FLESH |

Instead of attempting to reconcile in our minds Jesus Christ's divine and human natures, we simply need to accept Him the way He is portrayed in the Scripture. This is an integral part of true Christian faith. Coming in contact with this incomprehensible truth brings us first into a state of humble worship and amazement and then to a place of trust and obedience. All the commandments and rules, all ceremonies and rites, all ministry and missionary work lose their meaning without a vibrant realization of this reality.

The truth humbles

We live based on the assumption that we should be able to comprehend everything. Yet, when it comes face to face with God's incarnation, we see clearly only one thing: We cannot comprehend anything. Divine incarnation humbles us in a massive way!

> The Almighty — we cannot find him [some translations: "we cannot comprehend Him"]; he is great in power; justice and abundant righteousness he will not violate. **Therefore men fear him; he does not regard any who are wise in their own conceit."** (Job 37:23–24)

Notice the first thought in this verse — "We cannot find Him," or "cannot comprehend Him" — followed by a conclusion — "therefore…" For the very reason that we cannot comprehend Him fully, "therefore men fear Him." Fear or humility — this is the right way to respond to the inconceivability of God — because "He does not regard any who are wise in their own conceit."

The unity of the divine and human natures of Christ makes evident our helplessness and dependence on God. We begin to realize that He is much more intelligent, more powerful, and of a much higher order than us. He really is in charge in this world, and His ways are not our ways. He does what He believes is right, and He does not need our advice.

The truth inspires admiration

Christ's divine-and-human nature reveals the greatness of God's personality and amazes us. When we meditate on it, something wonderful happens: The concept of Christ's divine humanity brings us into a state of unspeakable joy. And it is not some artificial, unreasonable joy. We are astonished and overjoyed at the inconceivability of God's accomplished solutions!

God did not work the miracle of divine incarnation just to show off His abilities. The Son of God did not become man for the sake of an experiment. He did so because that was the only way to save you and me — which is amazing!

What gives us a sense of wonder is that the Father took His blameless Son and poured out upon Him all the horror of God's righteous wrath because our sins, yours and mine, were laid upon Him.

> For our sake he made him to be sin who knew no sin, so that in him we might become the righteousness of God. (2 Cor. 5:21)

The Mystery of Divine Incarnation | 63

How could this be: The Holy One suffers while the sinners are saved? How is it even possible for someone to pay our debts? We sinned, and He pays for it? This is not fair!

Now don't we admire the fact that God, clothed in flesh, gave us His righteousness? The fact that He did not merely make men His creation, but also His children?

Unfortunately, for many, these truths have become too trivial, completely uninspiring.

The book of Isaiah has a wonderful chapter that expresses this amazement at God's redemption plan. There the prophet exalts God's sovereignty in poetic form.

> Who has believed what he has heard from us?
> (Isa. 53:1–2)

Isaiah begins by saying, "What I am about to tell you is beyond real! If someone hears it, they will simply not believe it!"

> Who has believed what he has heard from us?
> And to whom has the arm of the Lord been
>   revealed?
> For he grew up before him like a young plant,
>   and like a root out of dry ground;
> he had no form or majesty that we should look
>   at him, and no beauty that we should desire him.
> (Isa. 53:1–2)

Isaiah is shocked: "Who would have thought that this is the Messiah? No pomp, no honors, no cherubim all around. He is weak, humiliated, so disfigured that the very sight of Him inspires disgust.

> He was despised and rejected by men,
>   a man of sorrows and acquainted with grief;
> and as **one from whom men hide their faces**
>   he was despised, and we esteemed him not. (Isa. 53:3)

This makes no sense! How could God allow Himself to be humiliated to the point where people look at Him with disdain? However, what follows takes the picture beyond our ability to comprehend.

> Surely he has **borne our griefs**
>   **and carried our sorrows**.

And then immediately,

> We esteemed him stricken,
>   smitten by God, and afflicted.
>
> But he was pierced for our transgressions;
>   he was crushed for our iniquities;
> upon him was the chastisement that brought
>   us peace,
>   and with his wounds we are healed. (Isa. 53:4–5)

Isaiah refuses to say that he comprehends everything God is doing. He merely records, as a court reporter, what is taking place. He sees Christ's emotions. He sees the motive behind His sacrifice.

> Out of the anguish of **his soul he shall see and be satisfied**;
> by his knowledge shall the righteous one,
>   my servant,
>   **make many to be accounted righteous,**
>   **and he shall bear their iniquities.**
> (Isa. 53:11)

Messiah will be satisfied with the results of His actions. Divine incarnation, the anguish of death that goes with it, the redemption of mankind — all this will bring Him joy and satisfaction. The mission will be accomplished: "Many" will be accounted righteous and their sins forgiven.

Moreover, Isaiah realizes that the results of Christ's actions will be equally pleasing to the Father.

> Yet it was **the will of the Lord** to crush him;
>   he has put him to grief;
> when his soul makes an offering for guilt,
>   he shall see his offspring; he shall prolong his days;
> the will of the Lord shall prosper in his hand.
> (Isa. 53:10)

The redemption of your soul and of mine is the most breathtaking feat in the universe! The plans thought out and enacted by God Himself — real love, tangible sacrifice — this causes admiration! So, it makes sense that

Paul, talking about salvation, can't help but admire its mystery and greatness:

> Oh, the depth of the riches and wisdom and knowledge of God! How unsearchable are his judgments and how inscrutable his ways!
>
> "For who has known the mind of the Lord,
>   or who has been his counselor?"
> "Or who has given a gift to him
>   that he might be repaid?"
>
> For from him and through him and to him
> are all things. To him be glory forever. Amen
> (Rom. 11:33–36)

The apostle realizes that God and His actions are so lofty that they are unattainable for the human mind. And Paul is overjoyed because God finds solutions which seem impossible to us.

The truth causes trust

The inconceivability of Christ's divine-and-human nature humbles the soul, overwhelms the mind, and inspires awe at God's amazing solutions. It is the most vivid revelation of God's love and faithfulness to His children.

When we realize that God loves us deeply and is willing to act when everything seems lost, we are filled with life-giving hope. His mind and power are far above us — so, we are safe to depend on Him. The Lord has timely and unexpected answers for every single situation in our lives.

God's fatherhood gives us assurance and confidence in life's trials. We are objects of His never-ending care.

If we try to take control over our lives, we are forced to admit we are powerless. Think of a woman carrying a child: She's entirely incapable of controlling the functions of her brain to send precise, timely commands to her own body to help the tiny human inside of her form properly and come into this world at the right time. In the same way, we have to admit that our ability to control the world is an illusion. But right on the heels of this realization, we find comfort because our lives are in the hands of a good God.

Comforting the people of Israel, Isaiah pointed out specifically the fact of God's inconceivability.

When it seems that there is no way out, when our mind finds no reason to hope for the better, we can remain calm and confident — trusting God.

> Lift up your eyes on high and see:
>   who created these?
> He who brings out their host by number,
>   calling them all by name;
> by the greatness of his might
>   and because he is strong in power,
>   not one is missing.
>
> Why do you say, O Jacob,
>   and speak, O Israel,
> "My way is hidden from the Lord,
>   and my right is disregarded by my God"?

> Have you not known? Have you not heard?
> The Lord is the everlasting God,
>   the Creator of the ends of the earth.
> He does not faint or grow weary;
>   **his understanding is unsearchable.**
>
> He gives power to the faint,
>   and to him who has no might he increases strength.
> Even youths shall faint and be weary,
>   and young men shall fall exhausted;
> **but they who wait for the Lord shall renew
>   their strength;**
> **they shall mount up with wings like eagles;**
> **they shall run and not be weary;**
>   **they shall walk and not faint.** (Isa. 40:25–31)

Notice the connection between the words "his understanding is unsearchable" and "they who wait for the Lord." We can wait on the Lord and trust Him. Why? Because He knows better than us! He is stronger than us! He has many more options!

Paul talks about the same thing in the book of Romans. In chapter 7 he describes the immense struggle that every child of God experiences, including himself — the struggle against our own flesh. Under the pressure of fleshly desires, the apostle cries out, "Wretched man that I am! Who will deliver me from this body of death?" But then chapter 8 is dripping with the soothing oil of words of comfort.

> What then shall we say to these things? If God is for us, who can be against us? (Rom. 8:31)

The Mystery of Divine Incarnation | 69

Where does Paul see God's protection? In the very fact of the divine humanity of Christ.

> He who did not spare his own Son but gave him up for us all, how will he not also with him graciously give us all things? (Rom. 8:32)

The reason the Father gave His Son was that salvation by good works and lifelong striving is severely lacking in God's eyes. However, God is an expert in impossible situations! He provided a way for us before our ancestors were even born and before the Fall of man happened. The plan of salvation was conceived a long time prior to all that.

> …knowing that you were ransomed from the futile ways inherited from your forefathers, not with perishable things such as silver or gold, but with the precious blood of Christ, like that of a lamb without blemish or spot.
>
> He was foreknown before the foundation of the world but was made manifest in the last times for the sake of you who through him are believers in God, who raised him from the dead and gave him glory, so that your faith and hope are in God. (1 Pet. 1:18-21)

If God loves us so much that He made the impossible possible by sending His Son in the flesh and allowing Him to die in our place, how can we doubt that He will find a way to solve even our most complicated problems? This is Paul's principal argument. This is the focal point of his trust.

Christ's divine humanity gives us yet another reason to be confident in God's favor to us. Jesus died, but He also rose from the dead and now sits at the right hand of the heavenly Father to intercede for every one of us.

> Who shall bring any charge against God's elect? It is God who justifies.
>
> Who is to condemn? Christ Jesus is the one who died — more than that, who was raised — who is at the right hand of God, who indeed is interceding for us.
>
> Who shall separate us from the love of Christ? Shall tribulation, or distress, or persecution, or famine, or nakedness, or danger, or sword? (Rom. 8:33–35)

After our every sin, our every trespass, all our imperfections, God-Man Jesus Christ reminds the Father of His perfect righteousness credited to us.

This means that when we come to God we may depend on resurrection and eternal life with Him. We may know Him as the Lamb who was slain for us personally[1]. We may depend on Christ to intercede for us when we repent of our sins. And we may stand forgiven and refreshed in God's grace and in strength for victory. We may read the final chapters of Revelation as our story.

---

[1] Rev. 5:9

Truth cultivates obedience

Divine revelation is the result of heavenly logic that far exceeds man's analytical skill.

As a matter of fact, there are many things in the world that we do not understand. Yet we don't feel ashamed about it. Do you understand the inner workings of a TV? The vast majority of people only know to push a certain button to watch the news. This is why instruction manuals are written — for those who don't have the foggiest idea about diodes, electrodes, transistors, and other things that make up the inner contents of that box.

So, God warns us: "Do not try to fully comprehend divine humanity! Accept what I tell you, and you will be blessed!" This is one of the reasons the Bible was given to us — as an instruction manual for living this life.

> "The secret things belong to the Lord our God, but the things that are revealed belong to us and to our children forever, that we may do all the words of this law." (Deut. 29:29)

God planned ahead to reveal to us exactly what we need to know to live as we should.

People would actually abandon all faith in the Lord in frustration if His revelation had contained only the incomprehensible thoughts and concepts of God. Recall a brief exchange in Christ's conversation with Nicodemus, a representative of the Jewish religious elite. Nicodemus was a member of the Sanhedrin, a group of individuals extremely well-versed in the Law, authorized to issue religious decrees of the highest order.

> Jesus answered, "Truly, truly, I say to you, unless one is born of water and the Spirit, he cannot enter the kingdom of God." ...
>
> Nicodemus said to him, "How can these things be?"
>
> Jesus answered him, "**Are you the teacher of Israel and yet you do not understand these things?** Truly, truly, I say to you, we speak of what we know, and bear witness to what we have seen, but you do not receive our testimony.
>
> **If I have told you earthly things and you do not believe, how can you believe if I tell you heavenly things?** No one has ascended into heaven except he who descended from heaven, the Son of Man. (John 3: 5, 9–13)

Nicodemus gave up when faced with God's wisdom.

Have you read passages in the Scripture that were difficult for you to comprehend? Now just imagine if God spoke to you in *only* such language!

We have to admit that when we come face to face with God, we encounter the inconceivable. We will never be able to encompass all His being with our minds. We will never be able to fully explain all the reasons of His actions. Yet, in spite of this, we need to walk in obedience to Him.

The Mystery of Divine Incarnation

So, our task is not to attempt to explain the inconceivable. Our task is to accept the reality of God. He took the steps necessary to reveal the truth to us by setting it forth in simple-to-understand terms, and our blessing is in building our life upon this truth.

> These are written so that you may believe that Jesus is the Christ, the Son of God, and that by believing you may have life in his name. (John 20:31)

I would like for you to approach this book as an opportunity to ponder the Messiah. As a chance to contemplate His humanity, His divinity, His suffering, and His sacrifice. As an opportunity to see in Him the Savior who solved in a very unique way the problem of your entirely real sin. As a chance for God to touch your soul and make it tremble before the divine.

WHAT DO *YOU* THINK OF CHRIST?

- Do you even think of Christ? And if so, what feeds your thoughts?

- What is your response to the divine humanity of Christ, and to your inability to fully grasp this fact?

- What is your religion built on? What is its cornerstone?

- How is your commitment to worshipping God manifested practically in the events of every day, week, year? How should it be expressed by the end of your life?

CHAPTER II
BORN TO DIE

Worthy is the Lamb who was slain,
to receive power and wealth and
wisdom and might and honor and
glory and blessing! | Rev. 5:12

| THE STORY
OF THE LAMB |

The Bible is a collection of 66 books. It has some 40 human authors and was written over more than 1,500 years. Its chapters are characterized by several different genres and styles. It covers a wide range of topics. But, despite the variety, if you analyze the Bible, you will very soon discover that it has an obvious, unifying theme and a common purpose.

The principal character in the Bible is God — Who saves mankind from eternal damnation and creates His church. From the first page of the book of Genesis to the last page of the book of Revelation, God progressively reveals to us His magnificent plan of salvation with Jesus Christ as the protagonist.

The Bible is a history book, a book on the history of humanity. It begins with the creation of man and ends with his glorification through unbreakable and eternal unification with God.

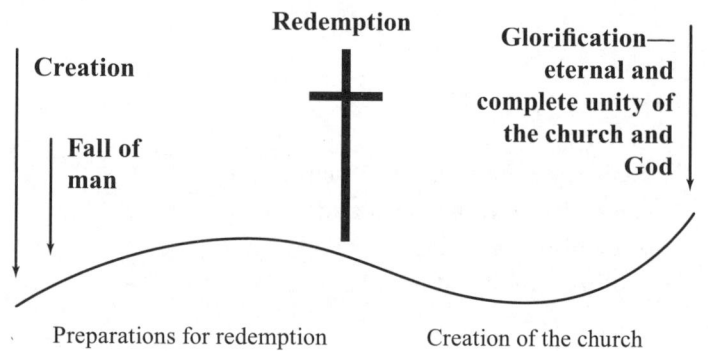

Universal History
Image 1

Prior to the creation described in the book of Genesis, the only One in existence was God. Then for a certain period — which we are now in — the material universe exists as well. But one day, the universe will reach a critical point: The church will be removed from this earth, and every human life will be scrutinized and summed up on the Judgment Day.

After that judgment, everything will be as it was before — the eternal God, existing by and of Himself. But there will be one substantial addition: From then on, the redeemed church will forever dwell in His presence.

The redemption achieved by the Son of God is the central point in human history (see Image 1). Everything that happened prior to that was preparation for the redemption and is described in the 39 books of the Old Testament.

But the apex of the Bible is found in the Gospels that contain descriptions of the birth, life, death, and resurrection of Christ — the principal elements of redemption. The other books of the New Testament are devoted to the formation of the church and lead on to the future, culminating with the triumphal banquet of the Lamb.

The events of world history, the resources of the universe, scientific achievements, human relationships — all this is just the scaffolding behind which the true masterpiece is being created, "the dwelling place of God with men.²"

Every detail of God's plan of building His church is painstakingly thought out. Nothing is unnecessary. With one divine thought, thousands of isolated elements are arranged into one chain in history, accomplishing several goals at once.

Yet the decisive move is still the coming of Jesus Christ, God in human form, to this earth. This is why Jesus Christ Himself emphasized time and again that all the Scripture in the Old Testament pointed to Him as the lead actor in human history.

---

[2] Rev. 21:3

> And he said to them,
>
> "O foolish ones, and slow of heart to believe all that the prophets have spoken! Was it not necessary that the Christ should suffer these things and enter into his glory?"
>
> And beginning with Moses and all the Prophets, he interpreted to them in all the Scriptures the things concerning himself. (Luke 24:25–27)

What was it that the "foolish and slow of heart" disciples were incapable of understanding? How exactly was it "necessary that the Christ should suffer these things and enter into his glory"?

Talking about the Messiah, the Old Testament repeatedly calls Him the Redeemer of Adam's descendants. The redemption of mankind, the most important spiritual transaction in the universe, took place at the moment when the blameless Son of God, clothed in human flesh, died as punishment for the sins of humanity. In that moment the totality of our sins was credited to His account; His death became the payment for our vice-filled lives; and His holiness was given to us. It is for this reason that we talk about the blameless Sacrifice as the central point in God's plan.

> And if you call on him as Father who judges impartially according to each one's deeds, conduct yourselves with fear throughout the time of your exile, knowing that you were ransomed from the futile ways inherited from your forefathers, not with

> perishable things such as silver or gold, but with the precious **blood of Christ, like that of a lamb without blemish or spot.**
>
> **He was foreknown before the foundation of the world** but was made manifest in the last times for the sake of you who through him are believers in God, who raised him from the dead and gave him glory, so that your faith and hope are in God. (1 Pet. 1:17–21)

This is why the Bible, on the grand scale, is the story of the Lamb. And this is why our own story is the story of the Lamb.

The Eternal Lamb

We lack the time to analyze all the passages speaking prophetically of the Messiah as the Lamb of God. As we dwell only on several key verses, even these will be enough to demonstrate the incredible meaning that God incorporated into the idea of sacrifice.

The story of the Lamb has an unusual beginning. As we have already noted, the Lamb was "foreknown" before the foundation of the world, meaning that when God created men, He already had before Him the entire plan of the development of the universe. He knew of the coming fall of man, and He realized there would be a need for a Redeemer. This is why He predetermined the Lamb for Himself.

> …**even as he chose us in him before the foundation of the world,** that we should be holy and blameless before him.

> In love he **predestined us for adoption** to himself as sons **through Jesus Christ**, according to the purpose of his will, to the praise of his glorious grace, with which he has blessed us in the Beloved.
>
> In him we have redemption through his blood, the forgiveness of our trespasses, according to the riches of his grace. (Eph. 1:4–7)
>
> For **those whom he foreknew he also predestined to be conformed to the image of his Son**, in order that he might be the firstborn among many brothers. And those whom he predestined he also called, and those whom he called he also justified, and those whom he justified he also glorified. (Rom. 8:29–30)

In other words, the story of redemption was tied from the very beginning to the second Person of the Trinity. God's solution was not improvised. Jesus Christ was chosen to be the key link in the cause of adoption long before the future sons and daughters came into this world.

In Chapter 3 of the book of Genesis, right after the fall, we find the first statement of the Redeemer. The situation did not catch God off guard: He sets forth the plan of how the spiritual catastrophe that just transpired would be remedied.

> The Lord God said to the serpent,
> "Because you have done this,
>   cursed are you above all livestock
>   and above all beasts of the field;

> on your belly you shall go,
>   and dust you shall eat
>   all the days of your life.
>
> **I will put enmity** between you and the woman,
>   and **between your offspring and her offspring;**
> **he shall bruise your head,**
>   **and you shall bruise his heel."** (Gen. 3:14–15)

Even though the word "Lamb" is not used in this text, He is surely the One referenced. He is that powerful seed of the woman that would smite Satan.

The seed of the woman sounds like an oxymoron to the modern ear. But that is the very essence of it: The Redeemer would be a descendant of a woman, to be accomplished much later by supernatural conception.

All the history that follows in the Old Testament is the necessary preparation for the act of sacrifice of this Lamb. Even without a degree in theology, we can notice several elements of this plan: the birth of the people of Israel, the Law given to it, humanity discovering its inability to keep the Law, the promise of the New Testament, and its establishment.

The lamb offered in Isaac's place

Several hundred years after the first prophecy of the Messiah, the Scriptures introduce us to the family of Abraham — the man whose seed was to become a blessing to all men according to the promise given to him by God.

Abraham and Sarah received an heir in their older years. They had waited for him long and hard. But when this son Isaac was in his teenage years, God unexpectedly ordered Abraham to sacrifice this heir.

This was a bizarre command — a command that broke Abraham's heart. Nevertheless, trusting God, the patriarch chose obedience. He had already learned the lesson that God's instructions are always the surest course of action, no matter how hard they may seem at first.

Not seeing any human way to reconcile the God-given promise to raise a great nation through Isaac with the order to kill him, Abraham presumed that God would raise Isaac from the dead and keep His promise this way[3]. So he went to Mount Moriah and prepared his son for sacrifice. At the last moment, God stopped the patriarch and substituted a lamb for Isaac:

> He said, "Do not lay your hand on the boy or do anything to him, for now I know that you fear God, seeing you have not withheld your son, your only son, from me."
>
> And Abraham lifted up his eyes and looked, and behold, behind him was a ram, caught in a thicket by his horns. And Abraham went and took the ram and offered it up as a burnt offering instead of his son. (Gen. 22:12–13)

---

[3] "By faith Abraham, when he was tested, offered up Isaac, and he who had received the promises was in the act of offering up his only son, of whom it was said, 'Through Isaac shall your offspring be named.' He considered that God was able even to raise him from the dead, from which, figuratively speaking, he did receive him back." (Heb. 11:17–19)

This amazing story does not merely demonstrate Abraham's faith. It also indicates the concept of a man being replaced by a lamb. Just like Isaac, sinful humanity has to die. Just like the lamb, the Messiah was prepared by God. Like the lamb who died in Abraham's son's place, the Lamb of God died for all of His spiritual children. But this is not all: Mount Moriah is the place where Jerusalem was later built. And it was here that the greatest sacrifice in the universe was offered.

The lamb slain instead of Jewish firstborn

The next significant mention of the Lamb is found in the story of Israel's exodus from Egypt.

After numerous plagues on the empire, due to the pharaoh's refusal to let Israel go, God prepared a final judgment. The night before the Jews left Egypt, a destroyer angel was designated to walk from house to house, killing every firstborn — both human and cattle. In order to safeguard the people of Israel, God ordered every family to slay a lamb and anoint the doorframe with its blood:

> Then Moses called all the elders of Israel and said to them,
>
> "Go and select lambs for yourselves according to your clans, and kill the Passover lamb. Take a bunch of hyssop and dip it in the blood that is in the basin, and touch the lintel and the two doorposts with the blood that is in the basin.
>
> None of you shall go out of the door of his house until the morning. For the Lord will pass through to

> strike the Egyptians, and **when he sees the blood on the lintel and on the two doorposts**, the Lord will pass over the door and will not allow the destroyer to enter your houses to strike you.
>
> You shall observe this rite as a statute for you and for your sons forever. (Exod. 12:21–24)

"The Lord will pass over…." Why? Because a lamb died in this house. But wherever there was no shedding of the blood of a lamb, the firstborn died.

From that time on, God commanded Israel to celebrate the Passover every year as a reminder of the Lamb Who was one day to die for all men, shielding them from the destroyer. Paul would later connect these two events.

> For Christ, our Passover lamb, has been sacrificed. (1 Cor. 5:7).

The lamb in the book of Isaiah

The most vivid image of the Redeemer as the Lamb is presented by Isaiah. This astonishing chapter, written 700 years prior to the birth of Jesus Christ, is the prophetic testimony to the Messiah's redeeming sacrifice.

> For he grew up before him like a young plant,
>   and like a root out of dry ground;
> he had no form or majesty that we should look
>   at him,
>   and no beauty that we should desire him.

He was despised and rejected by men,
   a man of sorrows and acquainted with grief;
and as one from whom men hide their faces
   he was despised, and we esteemed him not.

Surely he has borne our griefs
   and carried our sorrows;
yet we esteemed him stricken,
   smitten by God, and afflicted.

But he was pierced for our transgressions;
   he was crushed for our iniquities;
upon him was the chastisement that brought us peace,
   and with his wounds we are healed.

All we like sheep have gone astray;
   we have turned — every one — to his own way;
and the Lord has laid on him
   the iniquity of us all.

He was oppressed, and he was afflicted,
   yet he opened not his mouth;
like a lamb that is led to the slaughter,
   and like a sheep that before its shearers is silent,
      so he opened not his mouth.

By oppression and judgment he was taken away;
   and as for his generation, who considered
that he was cut off out of the land of the living,
   stricken for the transgression of my people?

Yet it was the will of the Lord to crush him;
   he has put him to grief;
when his soul makes an offering for guilt,
   he shall see his offspring; he shall prolong his days;
the will of the Lord shall prosper in his hand.

> Out of the anguish of his soul he shall see
>   and be satisfied;
> by his knowledge shall the righteous one,
>   my servant,
>   make many to be accounted righteous,
>   and he shall bear their iniquities.
>
> Therefore I will divide him a portion with the many,
>   and he shall divide the spoil with the strong,
> because he poured out his soul to death
>   and was numbered with the transgressors;
> yet he bore the sin of many,
>   and makes intercession for the transgressors.
> (Isa. 53:2–8, 10–12)

This passage contains an enormous number of facts concerning the Messiah. First, it is said here that Israel would not recognize her Redeemer: "We esteemed him not."

We also find multiple references to the substitutionary character of Christ's sacrifice: "He was pierced for *our transgressions*; he was crushed for our iniquities; upon him was the chastisement that brought *us* peace, and with his wounds *we are healed*... The Lord has laid on him the iniquity of *us all*... Stricken for the transgression *of my people*... When his soul makes an *offering for guilt*... *make many to be accounted righteous*, and he shall *bear their iniquities*... *makes intercession* for the transgressors." Substitution is what the Lamb's mission was all about.

Just like the lamb that replaced Isaac, human-replacing sacrifice would be selected and provided for by God

Himself: "Yet it was *the will of the Lord* to crush him; *he has put him* to grief."

Justification through this sacrifice will only be available through the knowledge of the Messiah: "By his knowledge shall the righteous one, my servant, make many to be accounted righteous, and he shall bear their iniquities."

This is the prophecy pertaining to the future repentance of Israel. One day, they will look at what they have done and be terrified. They will recognize their Lamb.

The lamb in the book of Zechariah

Another mention of sacrificing the Lamb is found in the book of Zechariah. This prophet writes about Israel's repentance that will take place in the days of the great Tribulation.

> And I will pour out on the house of David and the inhabitants of Jerusalem a spirit of grace and pleas for mercy, so that, when they look on me, on him whom they have pierced, they shall mourn for him, as one mourns for an only child, and weep bitterly over him, as one weeps over a firstborn.
>
> On that day the mourning in Jerusalem will be as great as the mourning for Hadad-rimmon in the plain of Megiddo. The land shall mourn.... (Zech. 12:10–12)

These words were written several centuries before crucifixion was even invented as a style of execution. God speaks about a special movement of the Spirit of God in the hearts of the remnant of Israel: the sight of the One they pierced will bring the nation to repentance.

The testimony of the forerunner concerning the Lamb

Shortly before Jesus Christ started His ministry, a messenger was sent before Him. The task of John the Baptist was to prepare the hearts of men and women through his preaching for the arrival of the Messiah, stirring in them the spirit of repentance.

John knew he was Christ's forerunner. Preparing the way for the Son of God was the goal of his life. The moment when revival in Israel reached its peak, the prophet presented the Messiah to the world.

It is striking that at this moment John, being filled with the Holy Spirit, referred to Jesus not as the King or Teacher, but specifically as the Lamb. This title conveyed His principal mission here on earth.

> The next day he saw Jesus coming toward him, and said,
>
> "Behold, the Lamb of God, who takes away the sin of the world! This is he of whom I said, 'After me comes a man who ranks before me, because he was before me.' I myself did not know him, but for this purpose I came baptizing with water, that he might be revealed to Israel." (John 1:29–31)

Assuming the role of the Lamb

Throughout His life on earth, Jesus repeatedly stated that the goal of His coming was to become the redemptive sacrifice for the sins of mankind. We will look at the two most vivid examples of His statements about this purpose.

The first is when Christ explains to the disciples the true meaning of greatness expressed in service.

> But Jesus called them to him and said,
>
> "You know that the rulers of the Gentiles lord it over them, and their great ones exercise authority over them. It shall not be so among you.
>
> But whoever would be great among you must be your servant, and whoever would be first among you must be your slave, even as **the Son of Man came not to be served but to serve, and to give his life as a ransom for many**." (Matt. 20:25–28)

Christ makes a powerful statement: My purpose is not to reign. I came to die and thus redeem mankind.

When Jesus says "ransom," He uses the Greek word "loutron" that was part of slave-merchant vocabulary. This word characterized the economic and legal relationship between parties in a sales transaction. In order for a slave to be freed or to become the property of another master, a "loutron," or a ransom, had to be paid. Christ says that He came to pay this ransom to free us, slaves to sin. And the ransom is His life.

Another example of Christ talking in detail about His redemptive mission took place at the Passover supper before His death.

Like millions of Jews over thousands of years, that night Jesus and His disciples were eating a lamb that had been slain in remembrance of Israel's deliverance from their Egyptian captivity. The Passover supper could not be eaten arbitrarily; its order was prescribed in detail in the Law. Yet, right in the middle of the ceremony, Jesus suddenly changed the traditional process and said something that profoundly increased the significance of what was taking place.

> And he took bread, and when he had given thanks, he broke it and gave it to them, saying, "This is **my body, which is given for you**. Do this in remembrance of me."
>
> And likewise the cup after they had eaten, saying, "This cup that **is poured out for you is the new covenant in my blood**." (Luke 22:19–20)

In a surprise move, Jesus spoke about the New Covenant previously promised by God through the prophets[4] — a covenant that would be established by the shedding of the blood of a new, perfect Lamb in order to save His people once again, and would now save all from damnation.

The Lamb in the book of Revelation

We started our review of the Lamb with the book of Genesis and have now come to the last book, Revelation. What is described in it focuses in many ways on events in heaven and the atmosphere there.

---

[4] Jer. 31:31-33; 32:40; Ezek. 36:26-28

> Then I saw in the right hand of him who was seated on the throne a scroll written within and on the back, sealed with seven seals. And I saw a mighty angel proclaiming with a loud voice,
>
> "Who is worthy to open the scroll and break its seals?"
>
> And no one in heaven or on earth or under the earth was able to open the scroll or to look into it, and I began to weep loudly because no one was found worthy to open the scroll or to look into it. And one of the elders said to me,
>
> "Weep no more; behold, the Lion of the tribe of Judah, the Root of David, has conquered, so that he can open the scroll and its seven seals."
>
> And between the throne and the four living creatures and among the elders I saw **a Lamb standing, as though it had been slain**, with seven horns and with seven eyes, which are the seven spirits of God sent out into all the earth. And he went and took the scroll from the right hand of him who was seated on the throne. (Rev. 5:1–7)

"The Lamb that was slain" is exactly the name that citizens of heaven will call their Redeemer. In other words, this title is Jesus' name forever!

The Lamb's victory, power, and authority in heaven will be acknowledged by everyone without exception — both the Gentile church and the redeemed Jews. The Lamb has overcome and therefore is worthy to break the seals that open the way for God's judgment.

> And when he had taken the scroll, the four living creatures and the twenty-four elders fell down before the Lamb, each holding a harp, and golden bowls full of incense, which are the prayers of the saints. And they sang a new song, saying,
>
> "Worthy are you to take the scroll
>   and to open its seals,
> for you **were slain**, and by your blood
>   **you ransomed people for God**
>   from every tribe and language and people and nation,
> and you have made them a kingdom and priests
>   to our God,
>   and they shall reign on the earth." (Rev. 5:8–10)

This proclamation by the elders and the seraphim is seconded by all the holy angels and by every creature. It is quite obvious that the Lamb takes the central place in the universe.

> Then I looked, and I heard around the throne and the living creatures and the elders the voice of many angels, numbering myriads of myriads and thousands of thousands, saying with a loud voice,
>
> "Worthy is **the Lamb who was slain**, to receive power and wealth and wisdom and might and honor and glory and blessing!"
>
> And I heard every creature in heaven and on earth and under the earth and in the sea, and all that is in them, saying, "**To him who sits on the throne and to the Lamb** be blessing and honor and glory and might forever and ever!" (Rev. 5:11–13)

Additionally, when God's judgments begin pouring out on the earth, every person will recognize that he or she is dealing with the Lamb.

> Then the kings of the earth and the great ones and the generals and the rich and the powerful, and everyone, slave and free, hid themselves in the caves and among the rocks of the mountains, calling to the mountains and rocks,
>
> "Fall on us and hide us from the face of **him who is seated on the throne, and from the wrath of the Lamb.**" (Rev. 6:15–16)

The Son of God is called the Lamb in Revelation dozens of times. The theme of the Lamb dominates this section of Scripture. To the Lamb belongs the final victory over the devil and his armies.

> They will make war on the Lamb, and **the Lamb will conquer** them, for he is Lord of lords and King of kings, and those with him are called and chosen and faithful. (Rev. 17:12–14).

The last part of Revelation not only talks of Jesus Christ's great victory over the powers of darkness, but also His triumphant unification with the church — those for whom He became the sacrifice of redemption. And in these verses, He is also shown as the Lamb.

> Then I heard what seemed to be the voice of a great multitude, like the roar of many waters and like the sound of mighty peals of thunder, crying out,
>
> "Hallelujah! For the Lord our God the Almighty reigns. Let us rejoice and exult and give him the glory, for **the marriage of the Lamb** has come, and his Bride has made herself ready; it was granted her to clothe herself with fine linen, bright and pure" — for the fine linen is the righteous deeds of the saints.
>
> And the angel said to me, "Write this: Blessed are those who are invited to **the marriage supper of the Lamb**." And he said to me, "These are the true words of God." (Rev. 19:6–9)

This celebration will mark the beginning of redeemed mankind's eternal fellowship with God — a fellowship filled with peace and joy.

> And I heard a loud voice from the throne saying, "Behold, **the dwelling place of God is with man**. He will dwell with them, and they will be his people, and God himself will be with them as their God.
>
> He will wipe away every tear from their eyes, and death shall be no more, neither shall there be mourning, nor crying, nor pain anymore, for the former things have passed away." (Rev. 21:3–4)

The presence of the Lamb in heaven will be a determining factor. Paradise is where the Lamb dwells.

> And I saw no temple in the city, for **its temple is the Lord God the Almighty and the Lamb**. And the city has no need of sun or moon to shine on it, for the glory of God gives it light, and **its lamp is the Lamb**. But nothing unclean will ever enter it, nor anyone who does what is detestable or false, but only those who **are written in the Lamb's book of life**. (Rev. 21:22–23, 27)

The image of the Lamb presents a number of traits that help us comprehend God and the nature of His works.

- The Lamb is a symbol of the blameless nature of the Son of God.
- The Lamb is a symbol of Christ's absolute dependence on and submission to His Father.
- The Lamb is a symbol of Jesus' humility and acceptance of His destiny.
- The Lamb is a symbol of Christ's vicarious sacrifice.
- The Lamb is a symbol of salvation from sin.
- The Lamb is a symbol of victory and triumph.
- The Lamb is a symbol of glory.

> And I heard every creature in heaven and on earth and under the earth and in the sea, and all that is in them, saying, "**To him who sits on the throne and to the Lamb** be blessing and honor and glory and might forever and ever!" (Rev. 5:13)

As we can see, the Holy Scriptures emphasize from the first pages to the last that the Messiah is a Lamb. And that is why we say that the redemptive sacrifice on the cross of Calvary was the main purpose of His incarnation.

If we take a close look at the testimony of the Gospel writers, a peculiar detail surfaces: Not every one of them describes the birth of Jesus Christ, yet each of them talks of His death in great detail.

If you look at the ratio of the text of the four Gospels, you will notice something else: The events of the thirty-three years of Jesus' life take up two thirds of the volume of the Gospels. The remaining third is dedicated to just one week — the last one — of His life. Now compare: Thirty-three years versus one week! This obviously sheds light on something crucial. It indicates that the purpose of Christ's coming was to die for people's sins. The Holy Spirit is unequivocally putting special emphasis on what happened on the cross of Calvary.

And why so? Why is the Messiah's death so important? Why did He have to die at all and suffer such terrible agony? Didn't God have other means to save mankind? Why was this cup not taken from Christ?

Trust me, if there had been at least the slightest chance to save us by some other means, God would have used it. The Father emphasized over and over again that Jesus was His only begotten Son, which means His only, His beloved, the dearest to His heart! Yet to realize why it was necessary for Christ to suffer, we need to see the scale of the problem of sin the way God sees it.

The sin of the first people delivered a devastating blow to the very essence of human existence. Sin is not just something men commit — depravity is the state of our souls. As J.I. Packer justly remarks, seconding the words of St. Augustine, "We are not sinners because we sin; we sin because we are sinners.[5]"

Sin is incorporated into our very DNA. Sin fills every cell. Although it lives in the heart, its influence permeates all of our being. We are spiritually dead men and women from the moment we are born.

I once heard of experts attempting to grow human organs in laboratories to help accident victims. The scientists said that when they took a heart cell and caused it to multiply, the new cells began pulsating from the first second of their existence. It is an innate, genetic characteristic of heart cells to do this.

In the same way, as a result of the fall, every human cell is raving with rebellion against God. We want to live by ourselves, for ourselves, the way we want. We reject the very idea of God, if not in our minds, then at the basic level of our desires, emotions, and will. Not just a part of us fights for self-affirmation, but our entire being is

---

[5] Packer, J. I. (2013, 07 15). Original Sin: Depravity Infects Everyone. Retrieved from Monergism: https://www.monergism.com/original-sin-depravity-infects-everyone

self-focused. This deeply rooted desire for self and sin is in fact the greatest problem of mankind.

The Scripture says that human sinfulness calls for never-ending punishment from God. In order to solve our sin problem, it needs to be removed from us, extracted out of our every cell. But it is absolutely impossible, just as it is impossible to remove a cancerous tumor that has grown deep into vital organs. In such cases, doctors say that the cancer is inoperable, meaning the person cannot be saved: attempting to remove the cancer would force the doctors to remove that which ensures life. As a result, the patient would die.

So, just as it is impossible to extract cancer from human tissue without damaging the tissue itself, sin is also inseparable from the person carrying it. Such a person must die. Depravity makes punishment absolutely inevitable. God's holiness demands it. God's wrath satisfies this demand. God's judgment sentences man to endless dying without a way to bring a definitive end to one's existence! This fact may irritate or frighten us, yet it cannot be ignored.

It was for this reason that God had to give His Son. This is why divine incarnation was necessary. It was the only way to break the vicious cycle of sin and death.

And God is capable of doing what is impossible for anyone else.

Out of His incredible love for people, He made the greatest sacrifice by sending His Son to die for the sake of our salvation. In order to implement this plan, the incarnate Messiah had to meet several important criteria which we have already touched on in passing.

- The Messiah had to be a representative of mankind — a real man.
- He had to be absolutely holy, untouched by original sin.
- He had to be prepared to take on Himself the sins of mankind and die.
- He had to live a holy life to overcome death.

These criteria are a unique combination! Imagine that the Messiah becomes a representative of mankind. The first requirement would be met. And imagine He is absolutely pure — the second and the fourth would be met as well. But, being a man of flesh and blood, imagine that He refuses to take our sins on Himself! And, honestly, why should He? He resists evil and pain just like us. He has His own opinion of how He should live His life.

This is why all the talk about the obedience of Christ is not empty rhetoric, as if Christ simply could not act otherwise, as if He were a robot. In reality, meeting all these requirements in the person of the God-Man was virtually impossible except for a meticulous plan conceived by God.

We will talk in more detail about the life and resurrection of Jesus Christ in later chapters, but in this one we will focus on the first three criteria of the Messiah.

| BONE OF THEIR BONES |

The Messiah had to be a descendant of Adam in order to act on behalf of mankind.

God could have created man all anew — without sin. But in order for the Messiah to stand in place of sinful mankind, He had to be one of them — bone of their bones and flesh of their flesh.

The Scripture says that Adam was a representative of all mankind. When he sinned, we all sinned with him.

> Therefore, just as sin came into the world through one man, and death through sin, and so death spread to all men **because all sinned**. (Rom. 5:12)

This truth continues to confound many. People do not want to accept that all men and women, without exception, are born already lost, accomplished rebels against God. However, as we can see, human depravity is a fact of life. The idea of original sin is not unacceptable to us because it is not true, but because we want the spiritual world to work according to our rules.

The difficulty in accepting this passage is that people are not always able to see the full extent of their corruption. Not everyone commits all possible sins to the maximum possible extent. Depending on cultural differences, upbringing, economic status, geographic location, etc., every individual human being develops his or her own version of sinfulness. But it is still there. It is inside. It is only prevented from reaching the full extent of its manifestation by external limiting factors.

Just look at the history of civilizations. If mankind is not restrained, we always end in corruption and immorality. Why is it that no empire has ever soared to the heights of morality — only crashing down? Where does this tendency come from? From within! Why was it that as soon as Hitler legitimized the killing of people based on race, millions of Germans — and other ethnic groups as well — signed up as butchers in the new system? Why, in spite of the shocking cruelty of the torture and other atrocities, did only a small portion of that society stand against this murderous machine? It was because Hitler's plan approved what had been restrained by religious and social norms — a vicious nature, eager to be released.

Because humans are innately sinful, for the first two decades of the Soviet regime no one thought twice before telling on a family member or a neighbor. Because people are internally corrupt, homosexuality thrived in the Roman empire. Because of human depravity, cannibalism was widespread until Christianity reached those regions.

Even at the dawn of the human history, God had to shorten the average human lifespan. The first people lived long, but their immorality was growing exponentially, further pushing mankind into the nightmare of sin.

> When man began to multiply on the face of the land… the Lord said, "My Spirit shall not abide in [or: My Spirit shall not contend with] man forever, for he is flesh: his days shall be 120 years." (Gen. 6:1,3)

I sometimes hear people blaming their children's bad behavior on a bad environment. But we must remember that bad friends only speed up the processes already at work inside us. All of our evil flows from this rotten, corrupt nature. The Bible states this fact without any arguments: Adam sinned, and all sinned in him, and this is confirmed by the fact that everyone dies — without exception.

> For if, because of one man's trespass, **death reigned through that one man**, much more will those who receive the abundance of grace and the free gift of righteousness reign in life through the one man Jesus Christ.
>
> Therefore, as **one trespass led to condemnation for all men**, so one act of righteousness leads to justification and life for all men.
>
> For as by the **one man's disobedience the many were made sinners**, so by the one man's obedience the many will be made righteous. (Rom. 5:17–19)

So, when we talk of God delivering people from sin, a need arises for a sinless representative of mankind from whom a new race could be raised. The Messiah had to be a descendant of Adam, yet be undefiled by his ancestor's sin so that everyone born through Him could be undefiled as well.

Adam could not present such a man. He was physically unable to produce a single righteous person. The angels could not solve our sin problem, either. It could only be a man. And this is why only a God-Man could qualify for such a task.

The Messiah came to earth and became a *real, authentic man* — the child of a human, Mary — yet an absolutely *sin-free* man as a result of being conceived by the Holy Spirit.

> **Since therefore the children share in flesh and blood, he himself likewise partook of the same things**, that through death he might destroy the one who has the power of death, that is, the devil, and deliver all those who through fear of death were subject to lifelong slavery.
>
> **For surely it is not angels that he helps, but he helps the offspring of Abraham.** (Heb. 2:14–16)

THE SECOND ADAM

By becoming a representative of humanity, the Messiah started a new lineage.

> For there is one God, and there is **one mediator between God and men, the man Christ Jesus**, who gave himself as a ransom for all. (1 Tim. 2:5–6)

Discussing the doctrine of resurrection in 1 Corinthians, Paul emphasizes again Jesus as the representative of mankind.

> For as by a man came death, by a man has come also the resurrection of the dead. For as in Adam all die, so also in Christ shall all be made alive. But each in his own order: Christ the firstfruits, then at his coming **those who belong to Christ**. (1 Cor. 15:21–23).

Just like everyone born of Adam will surely die, everyone born of Christ will surely live! When a believer is born of Jesus, he or she becomes a carrier of His nature. And now, just like everyone born of the first Adam gravitates to sin, everyone born of the second Adam feels aversion toward it.

> No one born of God makes a practice of sinning, for God's seed abides in him; and he cannot keep on sinning, because he has been born of God. (1 John 3:9)

Thus, the Messiah had to be a true representative of mankind so that He could be, as the new Adam, the father of a renewed race of people born from God and free from sin.

> But the free gift is not like the trespass. For if many died through one man's trespass, much more have **the grace of God and the free gift by the grace of that one man Jesus Christ abounded for many.**

> And the free gift is not like the result of that one man's sin. For the judgment following one trespass brought condemnation, but the free gift following many trespasses brought justification. (Rom. 5:15–16)

ONE WHO CARRIED THE CURSE

The second reason the Messiah had to become a man was in order to take on Himself the sin of mankind. Man sinned, and man had to pay for it. (Remember "loutron"?) It was utterly impossible for an angel to replace a human on the cross of Calvary.

Sometimes when we think about salvation, we tend to oversimplify our problem. We think, "Why did God have to go through so much trouble with incarnation, redemption, sanctification, glorification?... Couldn't He have made it simple — just save us, and that's it? He is God, after all!" We see God as a magician of sorts who was able to create the universe out of nothing, and so we think He could have just solved this problem in a moment as well. He could have just spoken, and everything would be alright.

We are also used to a world where people sometimes agree to forgive others and choose not to recall the murder or theft they committed, because we know we're all sinners and no one is perfect. The problem is, when we talk about God's economy, nothing just goes away in that system. In the physical world, created by the same God, matter and energy don't disappear. They may change their state, but they continue to exist. In the same manner, nothing just disappears in the Lord's system of moral justice. If man has sinned, he must receive punishment. It is an integral feature of God's world in general. Our God is perfectly holy and just.

Sin is not just a trespass. Sin is the condition of the heart out of which a wicked act proceeds. And it is that disposition of the human soul that causes God's holiness to respond in such anger.

> Cursed be everyone who does not abide by all things written in the Book of the Law, and do them. (Gal. 3:10).

But sin is not measured in quantity or volume. We have already stated that even if we presume an improbable scenario where a man sinned once and only once in his entire life, that sin still testifies of his flawed moral nature. And this sinful nature must receive God's punishment of eternal death.

It is ironic that many people are outraged by this system of God's justice while at the same time they accept the rules for courtmartial for disobeying an order! We, on the other hand, are not just guilty of some petty sin. Every cell in our body is sinful beyond measure!

Besides, the Bible says, "Cursed is everyone who does not abide by all things" — which means, keeping absolutely every rule for our entire lives, and not just in outward acts but also in disposition of our hearts. Remember the words of Christ:

> "You have heard that it was said to those of old, 'You shall not murder; and whoever murders will be liable to judgment.' But I say to you that everyone who is angry with his brother will be liable to judgment...
>
> "You have heard that it was said, 'You shall not commit adultery.' But I say to you that everyone who looks at a woman with lustful intent has already committed adultery with her in his heart. (Mat. 5:21-22, 27–28).

No, God doesn't classify our deeds as petty sins, regular sins, and big sins. Were you inconsistent in your obedience? Did you not obey all things? Then you are cursed!

We as humans tend to rationalize: "Adultery — that's really bad. But if people lie or don't do something quite as they should, that's a much smaller sin. Does that mean they really have to be cursed? Everyone does that! Should we curse everyone then?"

That's the thing: You are absolutely right — everyone is cursed! This is the core of biblical teaching and the purpose of the Old Testament — to help people to realize their utter depravity and hopelessness. And for this reason, Jesus *had* to be absolutely holy in order to solve the problem of human sin.

Holy Man

Because each of us is born corrupt, we fail the qualifying contest: we're incapable of taking another person's sin on ourselves. Only someone who had no sin himself could take on someone else's transgression.

Let's compare this to AIDS. One who has been infected with AIDS once cannot get infected again. Even if the disease has not reached its advanced stages, the person is already a carrier of the virus which will gradually cause death. In the same way, a sinful person cannot die for someone else's wrong when he already carries his own guilt leading to eternal death.

This is one of the reasons why God had to become a holy and sinless man. The Messiah had to be blameless like a sacrificial lamb.

Reading the Old Testament, you see a repeated warning: "Your lamb shall be without blemish" (Exod. 12:5). There are roughly fifty statements about this. The Scripture deliberately emphasizes the blameless nature of Jesus Christ.

> For Christ also suffered once for sins, the **righteous** for the unrighteous, that he might bring us to God, being put to death in the flesh but made alive in the spirit. (1 Pet. 3:18)

Only one who was completely undefiled by own sin could bear the judgment of humanity.

> For our sake he made him to be sin **who knew no sin**, so that in him we might become the righteousness of God. (2 Cor. 5:21)

> Surely he has borne **our** griefs and carried **our** sorrows; yet we esteemed him stricken, smitten by God, and

> afflicted. But he was pierced for **our** transgressions; he was crushed for our iniquities; upon him was the chastisement that brought **us** peace, and with his wounds we are healed. (Isaiah 53:4–5)

So, to be able to carry the sin of mankind, the Messiah had to be a sinless man Himself. However, there is yet another important criterion: Christ did not merely have to be holy. He had to be infinite.

Infinite God

Did you ever experience your heart just being torn inside when you heard of someone committing some kind of horrible and violent act? Let's imagine that someone has severely abused multiple children and then murdered them. If you heard that the court sentenced the criminal to life imprisonment or even death, you'd naturally be outraged that the sin committed against those victims far exceeded the punishment. The penalty in no way equals the loss. It is impossible to pay with one death for the lives of many children!

But now consider this: man's sin is more than just wronging his peers. It's a crime against an infinite and perfectly holy God. This means that the punishment for it must be proportionate to the insult to the other party. The punishment must be eternal.

Imagine that a hacker attempts to get into his neighbor's personal email account that has no particular value. Of course, his actions are illegal, but the court will probably be lenient to such a person. But now assume that this same hacker uses the same method to get into the computer system of a national security agency. The measure of punishment won't be determined by the complexity of his hacking skills, but by the importance of the object he has attacked.

God's status is much higher than that of a national security system. God's power is absolute. God's attributes are superlative. He is eternal, holy, omnipresent, omniscient. He is infinitely greater than us. He is different from any other being. So it is a huge mistake to think that an eternal lake of fire is an unjust punishment for all who do not bow before Christ. It is completely fair! God is absolutely greater than us, and the guilt of such rebellion against God is immeasurable.

And *accepting* a punishment of such scale is a task that only someone infinite, someone absolutely holy, could perform. This is yet another reason why the Messiah had to be God. He had to have the ability to carry people's infinite guilt in the eyes of the Father. Peter talks about it, indicating the inconceivable price of our redemption:

> And if you call on him as Father who judges impartially according to each one's deeds, conduct yourselves with fear throughout the time of your exile, knowing that you were ransomed from the futile ways inherited from your forefathers, not with perishable things such as silver or gold, but **with the precious blood of Christ, like that of a lamb without blemish or spot. He was foreknown before the foundation of the world** but was made manifest in the last times for the sake of you. (1 Pet. 1:17–20)

The Messiah's suffering was infinite. Look at what Jesus Christ had to endure.

> Then the soldiers of the governor took Jesus into the governor's headquarters, and **they gathered the whole battalion before him.** And they **stripped him** and put a scarlet robe on him, and twisting together **a crown of thorns**, they put it on his head and put a reed in his right hand. And kneeling before him, they **mocked him**, saying, "Hail, King of the Jews!"
>
> And **they spit on him** and took the reed and **struck him on the head**. And when they **had mocked him**, they stripped him of the robe and put his own clothes on him and led him away to crucify him. (Matt. 27:27–31)

Imagine the vicious cruelty of a battalion of Roman soldiers — men who went down in history as having no conscience! Feel this pain. Try standing there, next to Jesus Christ, and look at the whip He is beaten with, the rod forcefully hitting His head, driving the thorns from the crown deeper and deeper.... This torture went on for quite some time. Isaiah says that no one ever was as humiliated as Christ.

> As many were astonished [horror-stricken] at you — **his appearance was so marred, beyond human semblance**, and his form beyond that of the children of mankind. (Isa. 52:14)

Even the people who yelled, "Crucify Him!" were horrified and disgusted at the sight of His disfigured face.

Listen to how David prophetically described His suffering:

> My God, my God, why have you forsaken me?
>   Why are you so far from saving me, from
>   the words of my groaning?
>
> O my God, I cry by day, but you do not answer,
>   and by night, but I find no rest.
>
> All who see me mock me;
>   they make mouths at me; they wag their heads;
> "He trusts in the Lord; let him deliver him;
>   let him rescue him, for he delights in him!"
>
> Yet you are he who took me from the womb;
>   you made me trust you at my mother's breasts.
> On you was I cast from my birth,
>   and from my mother's womb you have been my God.
> Be not far from me,
>   for trouble is near,
>   and there is none to help.
>
> Many bulls encompass me;
>   strong bulls of Bashan surround me;
> they open wide their mouths at me,
>   like a ravening and roaring lion.
>
> I am poured out like water,
>   and all my bones are out of joint;
> my heart is like wax;
>   it is melted within my breast;
> my strength is dried up like a potsherd,
>   and my tongue sticks to my jaws;
>   you lay me in the dust of death.

> For dogs encompass me;
>   a company of evildoers encircles me;
> they have pierced my hands and feet —
>   I can count all my bones —
> they stare and gloat over me;
>   they divide my garments among them,
>   and for my clothing they cast lots.
>
> But you, O Lord, do not be far off!
>   O you my help, come quickly to my aid!
> Deliver my soul from the sword,
>   my precious life from the power of the dog!
> Save me from the mouth of the lion!
> You have rescued me from the horns
>   of the wild oxen! (Ps. 22:1–2, 7–22)

He was not crucified with political prisoners; He was not given a more privileged place as someone dying for an idea. He was crucified with hardened criminals.

> He...was numbered with the transgressors; (Isa. 53:12)
>
> Then two robbers were crucified with him, one on the right and one on the left. (Matt. 27:38)

Were you ever accused of something you didn't do? Of having evil intentions you never had? How did you feel? But what would you feel if you were sentenced to death for that alleged crime? And what if you were executed by the person who was actually guilty of the crime you were accused of?

> And those who passed by derided him, wagging their heads and saying, "You who would destroy the temple and rebuild it in three days, save yourself! If you are the Son of God, come down from the cross." (Matt. 27:39–40)

People mocked His ability to work miracles. He did work miracles! They witnessed it. He could calm a storm. He could strike a crowd with blindness. Just a day before the attempt to arrest Him, "Jesus said to them, 'I am he,' [and] they…fell to the ground." And now they were challenging Him: "You don't have the power to raise yourself from the dead?" It is ridiculous.

> So also the chief priests, with the scribes and elders, mocked him, saying, "He saved others; he cannot save himself. He is the King of Israel; let him come down now from the cross, and we will believe in him. He trusts in God; let God deliver him now, if he desires him. For he said, 'I am the Son of God.'" (Matt. 27:39–43)

It had been a lengthy confrontation, and now it was reaching its peak. The Jewish rulers were under the impression that they had finally gotten control of this Teacher Who stood in their way. Now, they were in power, and they used it to the fullest.

Over the course of three and a half years people had turned to Christ, and the Pharisees had said, "No, He is not the One! You cannot believe Him! He is a false teacher! He comes from Satan!" People were healed, and the Pharisees would excommunicate them. Now they were delivering their final blow: "Come on — come down from the cross, and we will believe in You." And then they hit Him where it hurt the most: "He trusts in God; let God deliver him now, if he desires him. For he said, 'I am the Son of God.'"

There are types of moral humiliation that are more painful than physical suffering. But this an impossible combination of the two. Now, that is infinite suffering!

But the worst was yet to come.

Remember a situation where you felt unbearable pain. Remember when a friend betrayed you. Remember a misunderstanding with your family. Where did you go then? You ran to God.... It is the last resort a person has. When everyone has abandoned us, we can still pray and find comfort in the Lord. Our judicial system doesn't deny this even to criminals.

But Christ did not have such a chance. The Father turned His face away from Him! Jesus became the object of His wrath and judgment.

Any convict, even the worst of the worst, can withstand punishment because God's universal grace continues showing him a degree of mercy. Jesus Christ, however, experienced the entire gamut of suffering alone. The Father turned away from Him because He saw Jesus as the One guilty of our sin — yours and mine.

> Now from the sixth hour there was darkness over all the land until the ninth hour. And about the ninth hour Jesus cried out with a loud voice, saying, "Eli, Eli, lema sabachthani?" that is, "**My God, my God, why have you forsaken me?**" (Matt. 27:45–46)

None of us would be able to go through this!

Has it ever seemed to you that God has forsaken you? How horribly scared and lonely did you feel then? Christ did not imagine that His Father had forsaken Him — because the Father truly had! God the Father had turned His face away from Christ, closing His eyes and ears to Jesus' cries for help.

This is why only God incarnate — holy Man possessing infinite, divine patience — could save mankind!

ONE OF THE MORTALS

Our sin calls for punishment. And this punishment is death.

> For the wages of sin is death, but the free gift of God is eternal life in Christ Jesus our Lord. (Rom. 6:23)

To save people from their sin, it was necessary not only to suffer, but to die. Many people think that the trials they suffer in life can somehow atone for their guilt before God. This could not be further from the truth. The proportionate punishment for sin is death and eternal hell. And no human being could ever suffer through that.

As we have already gathered from the Scriptures, only absolute holiness could work in the context of man's salvation. So, no human being is able to carry the sin of humanity. Only God possesses this holiness. But God cannot die! Besides, God does not have to die because He does not sin.

This is a great conundrum for which God has provided a solution — what He calls the great mystery of godliness: God was manifested in the flesh! On Christmas night, the God-Man appeared on earth — One Who could carry the infinite guilt of human sin and Who could also die for it!

God had warned from the very beginning that sin inevitably leads to death.

> And the Lord God commanded the man, saying, "You may surely eat of every tree of the garden, but of the tree of the knowledge of good and evil you shall not eat, for in the day that you eat of it **you shall surely die**." (Gen. 2:16–17)

The reason for such a stern warning lies in God's holiness. God is totally intolerant of sin. He is incompatible with it in any shape or form. Everyone without exception who rebels against His holiness is invariably crushed by His wrath. This is why the words "you shall surely die" mean that man will absolutely certainly die without the slightest chance to avoid death. God's word comes true and never fails.

There is a saying also: "Everything is an illusion. Only death is real." Everyone realizes that death is an inescapable reality. You could immortalize your name, you could use others to further your goals, you could satisfy your every desire, but sooner or later you will have to die. Eventually, every human being will return to dust. And in the end, every person will have to stand before the Creator.

The Scripture talks about three aspects of death. The first one is spiritual death, which began immediately after man rebelled against God. Paul describes it in Ephesians:

> And you were **dead in the trespasses and sins** in which you once walked, following the course of this world, following the prince of the power of the air, the spirit that is now at work in the sons of disobedience— among whom we all once lived in the passions of our flesh, carrying out the desires of the body and the mind, and were by nature children of wrath, like the rest of mankind. (Eph. 2:1–3)

We are utterly incapable of demonstrating a level of kindness and holiness that would please God. We have been excluded as potential candidates for righteousness since our birth. Though we "live" for some time, we are spiritually dead already.

This first aspect of death is inevitably followed by the second one — physical death. A person eventually disintegrates and returns to dust. But for many people, there will also come an eternal death. The book of Revelation says,

> But as for the cowardly, the faithless, the detestable, as for murderers, the sexually immoral, sorcerers, idolaters, and all liars, their portion will be in the lake that burns with fire and sulfur, which is the second death. (Rev. 21:8)

This is why the Messiah did not only have to be punished for the sins of mankind, but also had to die. Paul presents the death of Jesus Christ as an integral part of the Good News:

> For I delivered to you as of first importance what I also received: that Christ died for our sins in accordance with the Scriptures. (1 Cor. 15:3)

This is the essence of the Gospel, friends. Christ was born in order to die. His death is not a mundane fact in His biography. It is the focal point of salvation. It was the very thing pointed out in Isaiah's prophecy:

> …that he was cut off out of the land of the living, **stricken** for the transgression of my people. (Isa. 53:8)

The author of Hebrews explains in detail how death is connected with the forgiveness of sin.

> Indeed, under the law almost everything is purified with blood, and **without the shedding of blood there is no forgiveness of sins.** Thus it was necessary for the copies of the heavenly things to be purified with these rites, but the heavenly things themselves with better sacrifices than these.
>
> For Christ has entered, not into holy places made with hands, which are copies of the true things, but into heaven itself, now to appear in the presence of God on our behalf. Nor was it to offer himself repeatedly, as the high priest enters the holy places every year with blood not his own, for then he would have had to suffer repeatedly since the foundation of the world.
>
> **But as it is, he has appeared once for all at the end of the ages to put away sin by the sacrifice of himself.** (Heb. 9:22–26)

Jesus Christ was born to die. This is the mystery of the divine incarnation. Salvation, yours and mine, is in His death.

> Though he was in the form of God, [he] did not count equality with God a thing to be grasped, but emptied himself, by taking the form of a servant, being born in the likeness of men. And being found in human form, he humbled himself **by becoming obedient to the point of death, even death on a cross.** (Phil. 2:6–8)

WHAT DO *YOU* THINK OF CHRIST?

- What is the standard you use to measure your sinfulness?

- Why does the Bible say that the punishment for your morally acceptable life is death and eternal hell?

- How has Christ manifested His complete identification with you in your personal guilt before God?

CHAPTER III
BORN TO LIVE

"For if while we were enemies, we were reconciled to God by the death of his Son, much more, now that we are reconciled, shall we be saved by his life."
| Rom. 5:10

Man's original sin called for punishment by death. Jesus Christ as mankind's blameless representative offered this redeeming sacrifice in our place. The death of the Son of God solved the problem of our guilt and afforded us the opportunity to live a new, holy life. However, the question remains: What next?

We easily discover that even after all Jesus has done for us, we are unable to live a perfect life that meets the highest standards of God's holiness. It is not just difficult, it is impossible!

Even the most sincere and zealous among God's children run constantly short of the level of holiness acceptable to God. Even when we try not to commit big sins, we are still not kind enough, not loving enough, not committed to God enough. Here and there we slip into laziness, immaturity, fear, offense, irritation… And even our good deeds do not always have pure motives. All of this is entirely unacceptable. God needs a perfect life!

This is why Jesus Christ came to earth as a baby. He walked the entire life's journey from birth to death in order to live a blameless human life that would be credited to all who by faith receive Him as their Savior and Lord. The Holy Scriptures emphasize this truth many times, but it is presented in the most detail and with the best clarity in Romans.

Having explained the need for Jesus Christ's vicarious death in chapter three of this epistle (Rom. 3:25), the apostle points out another aspect of salvation that is just as important — His vicarious life:

> But God shows his love for us in that while we were still sinners, Christ died for us. Since, therefore, we have now been justified by his blood, much more shall we be saved by him from the wrath of God.
>
> For if while we were enemies we were **reconciled to God by the death of his Son**, much more, now that we are reconciled, shall we **be saved by his life**. (Rom. 5:8–10)

This passage talks about the dual roles that Christ's righteousness plays in our salvation. The first aspect was demonstrated on Calvary when God placed our sin on His Son and subjected a blameless Victim to the punishment of death. This act frees us from sin.

But the second aspect of Christ's righteousness encompasses what happened before the cross of Calvary. God does not merely credit to our account the death of the Righteous One. He credits us with His righteous life as well. This is the reason that Christ needed to live His years on earth. And just like sin affects everyone born of Adam, everyone born of Jesus Christ will have life — guaranteed.

> Therefore, as one trespass led to condemnation for all men, so one act of righteousness leads to justification and life for all men. For as by the one man's disobedience the many were made sinners, so by the one man's obedience the many will be made righteous. (Rom. 5:18–19)

It is obvious that since man is saved by the Messiah's righteousness, the quality and quantity of his own works does not matter. Even if he is a saint to the maximum degree, he is still hopeless. The only way to salvation is to obtain the life of Christ.

> Jesus answered, "Truly, truly, I say to you, unless one is born of water and the Spirit, he cannot enter the kingdom of God." (John 3:5)

In Romans, the apostle Paul gives a more detailed picture of the depth of God's design, explaining how the righteousness of Jesus Christ shifted from potential to actual.

Due to His nature, the Messiah was always holy. But His righteousness had a practical manifestation in His obedience to the Father throughout His life on earth. Another passage describes this same concept:

> Although he was a son, he learned obedience through what he suffered. And being made perfect, he became the source of eternal salvation to all who obey him. (Heb. 5:8–9)

This idea naturally begs a question: If we are saved by the fact that Jesus' righteous life has been credited to our account, does that mean that our own life has no weight for eternity? Does that mean that any attempts at a holy life are pointless? Does that mean that we can live any way we want and still make it to heaven?

Paul anticipated this question and responds several times, in an emphatic and unequivocal way, to this flawed interpretation of this doctrine.

> What shall we say then? Are we to continue in sin that grace may abound? By no means! (Rom. 6:1-2)

Unfortunately, in translation the intensity of the emphasis of "by no means" is expressed too weakly for the modern reader to appreciate. These two Greek words "μὴ γένοιτο" use the form of utmost negation. Most English versions render it as, "May it never be!" — something to the effect of, "Such a thing is in no way possible!"

But many people do not hear this negation, and instead of accepting the truth of salvation through Christ's righteousness — clearly portrayed at the end of Romans 5 — they try to find a way to avoid it. It doesn't fit people's narrative to accept total dependence on what Christ did in our place and not on what we do ourselves. People think that this will allow universal license to sin, and to make sure that doesn't happen, they add a pinch of Law to grace.

In reality, there is no need for any of this. The Bible was not written for us to add something to it. The statement concerning salvation through Christ's righteousness, not through ours, makes sense in the context of what follows. In chapter 6, Paul explains why a person saved through the righteousness of the Son of God cannot tolerate sin under any circumstances.

> How can we who died to sin still live in it?
>
> Do you not know that all of us who have been baptized into Christ Jesus were baptized into his death?
>
> We were buried therefore with him by baptism into death, in order that, just as Christ was raised from the dead by the glory of the Father, we too might walk in newness of life. (Rom. 6:2–4)

Salvation implies a radical change in our attitude toward God's will: True believers hate sin and yearn for righteousness because there is a new nature present in them. That is why the very wording of the question, "Should we sin that grace may abound?" is absolutely unnatural for true Christians.

This being said, the apostle underlines yet another reality. Having been born again, God's children continue living in mortal bodies that gravitate toward sin. Even the most perfect and zealous Christians do not love the way they should. They take offence, are lazy, do not dedicate themselves to God enough... And the sensitive conscience of a righteous person will always be aware of imperfection. So, Paul dedicates the entire next chapter to the description of the spiritual war he is in. He is so desperate at times that he exclaims,

> For I do not do the good I want, but the evil I do not want is what I keep on doing.
>
> For I delight in the law of God, in my inner being, but I see in my members another law waging war against the law of my mind and making me captive to the law of sin that dwells in my members.
>
> Wretched man that I am! Who will deliver me from this body of death? (Rom. 7:19, 22–24)

If you are a true Christian, you have likely had similar experiences and felt those words. This same cry goes up from all souls weary of struggling with their own inadequacy. It is a serious challenge in the lives of all genuine Christians.

Nominal Christians — that is, those who have not experienced a genuine rebirth — get accustomed to sin. They don't care if their lives please God. Their level of tolerance to sin is high. This struggle is absent from their lives. They aren't concerned as they sin a little here and there, gradually getting used to an increasing level of corruption. They may feel remorse, yet not because they fall short of God's standards but because of social expectations. When evaluating their actions, they take into account what those surrounding them think. And if they do abandon sin, it's only because they feel uncomfortable among others.

However, if a person is a true believer, he hates sin because his heart is dedicated to God. Having evil tendencies in his own flesh, he lives in a state of constant struggle. Often the agony of this tension brings desperation, and he echoes the apostle's words that struggling is very hard.

Yet Paul does not merely describe the problem. He immediately goes on to talk about the hope Christ brought.

> Thanks be to God through Jesus Christ our Lord! (Rom. 7:25)

Paul thanks God, emphasizing that tension caused by the confrontation between the old sinful nature and the new man born of God is successfully solved by Jesus Christ.

> There is therefore now no condemnation for those who are in Christ Jesus. For the law of the Spirit of life has set you free in Christ Jesus from the law of sin and death. For God has done what the law, weakened by the flesh, could not do.

> By sending his own Son in the likeness of sinful flesh and for sin, he condemned sin in the flesh, in order that the righteous requirement of the law might be fulfilled in us, who walk not according to the flesh but according to the Spirit. (Rom. 8:1–4)

This text, seemingly complex at first glance, reveals the amazing riches hidden in the truth of the divine incarnation: Christ lived a human life…

- to make us righteous,
- for us to strive to live righteously,
- to give us an example of righteousness,
- and to become the Intercessor vindicating us.

MADE RIGHTEOUS BY THE LIFE OF CHRIST

Some people ask, "This struggle inside never ends — could that mean I'm not saved? Why do I feel like sleeping in more than going to church?" The answer is on the surface: You are undisciplined. You do not only feel like sleeping when it is time to go to church; you also feel like sleeping in when it is time to go to work. Still, you never wonder, "Perhaps I'm just not made for work." You realize that if you don't go to work, there will be no food on the table.

The basics are the same for spiritual life: If you don't go to church, you won't be spiritually healthy. And if you have a long day and go to bed at 12:30 in the morning, then yes, getting up for church will not be easy. The flesh has its own demands; however, the spirit can bring the flesh under submission. Paul does not tell us we will have no struggles. He does not promise that we will instantly break free of the imperfections of the flesh. He helps us to have the right perspective of the nature of this struggle.

> **There is therefore now no condemnation for those who are in Christ Jesus.** For the law of the Spirit of life has set you free in Christ Jesus from the law of sin and death. For God has done what the law, weakened by the flesh, could not do.
>
> By sending his own Son in the likeness of sinful flesh and for sin, he condemned sin in the flesh, in order that the righteous requirement of the law might be fulfilled in us, who walk not according to the flesh but according to the Spirit. (Rom. 8:1–4)

The apostle reminds us that being born from God, being born again, implies not only being joined to Him in the death of Jesus Christ, but also in His life. His (and that means *our*) righteous life is what grants us freedom from condemnation! Paul states this clearly: "There is now *no condemnation*." In Greek this sentence begins with the word "no," emphasizing the absolute nature of God's acceptance.

So, in spite of the struggle, in spite of our weariness, in spite of the fact that we are not always walking in victory, the life that God's children have in Jesus Christ sets them free from guilt. Paul indicates two reasons why this life is so powerful in believers.

The Man who fulfilled the Law

> Do not think that I have come to abolish the Law or the Prophets; I have not come to abolish them but to fulfill them. (Matt. 5:17)

This basic fact contains a truth of immeasurable significance: In becoming a man, Christ did actually overcome sin. He fulfilled all of the requirements of the Law:

> ...what the law, weakened by the flesh, could not do. (Rom 8:3)

The Law was given so that our depravity would become obvious to us. God, so to say, brought His standards from heaven to earth in order to show men that they can never live up to them. No one, even the most noble person, is able or willing to fulfill His righteous, just requirements.

The Law could not make humanity righteous. Therefore, God sent His Son to earth.

> For God has done what the law, weakened by the flesh, could not do. By sending his own Son in the likeness of sinful flesh. (Rom. 8:3)

Christ was born in flesh just like our own — same conditions, same reality, same limitations. Only one thing set Him apart from us: holiness. The rest was the same — desires, needs, will.

He felt like sleeping, especially in the morning. He wished to eat something tasty. He experienced cold and heat, needing a roof over His head the same way we do. He knew from experience what physical pain and weariness mean. Day after day he received thousands of people who could easily exhaust, irritate, hurt Him, and take up His precious time.

> And a scribe came up and said to him, "Teacher, I will follow you wherever you go."
>
> And Jesus said to him, "Foxes have holes, and birds of the air have nests, but the Son of Man has nowhere to lay his head." (Matt. 8:19−20)

Christ said, "Will you follow me? I am difficult to follow. I have nowhere to live, I often have no place to spend the night."

He came without sin. But the mystery is that He lived a life under the kind of pressure which inevitably causes us to give in, yet He remained without sin. Under these severe circumstances, Jesus Christ's potential righteousness was transformed into actual. That means that He acted in every situation the way that best pleased the Father. He lived a righteous life.

For us to fully comprehend this truth, we need to think back to the Garden of Eden.

Imagine a natural environment that is strikingly beautiful. No aggression or even the slightest lack of harmony can even be conceived of in this place. It is warm, fresh. The weather is perfect. Everything Adam and Eve need is available in abundance. No economic crisis, no problems with lack of sleep, no disease, no natural catastrophes. No death! More than that, there is no personal tension due to a presence of sin in the world and in the body. No relationship issues. Life is just perfect. And two perfect people, with no original sin, living under these perfect conditions, were still unable to withstand a temptation!

Now imagine yourself. You come to God, and through Christ's shed blood, He sets you free from sin and restores you to the state of Adam and Eve. But He leaves you to yourself to continue to live a pure and holy life, preserving your soul for the Kingdom of Heaven. Then, you keep finding yourself experiencing pain, a friend's betrayal, lack of work or overload. Increasing problems begin to weigh down even you, a sinless "Adam" or "Eve," living in our modern world. How long will you last before you yield to sin?

Today, it would be impossible for anyone to remain free from sin, even if they were made sinless again. That is why Satan felt triumphant after the fall of Adam and Eve. He was absolutely convinced that all mankind, when in difficult circumstances, will inevitably sin.

Remember the situation described in the book of Job (1:11, 2:5). God presented Satan with a question: "Have you considered my servant Job? Blameless? Upright?" And Satan counters, "Really? Upright? Just change his circumstances a little, and you will see the kind of man he is. This is nothing new — there were two just like him many years ago… They lived well, but then, You see, they fell.…"

The Person of Christ, God incarnate, left Satan wondering. Though the devil said to Jesus, "If you are the Son of God," he actually hoped He would be just like us, a man, and for this reason he tempted Him in the most elaborate ways. However, Christ's resistance to sin was absolutely surreal in the eyes of our archenemy.

> If you are the Son of God, command these stones to become loaves of bread. (Matt. 4:3)

Satan put Him in a position that exacerbated the ever-present desires of the flesh. Christ was extremely hungry already. He was incredibly tired. He had no energy, no strength. He was exhausted. And Satan was so confident of himself: In a situation like this, he thought, even the holiest of saints will sin.

> But he answered, "It is written,
>
> 'Man shall not live by bread alone,
>   but by every word that comes from
>   the mouth of God.'" (Matt. 4:4)

Instead of giving in to Satan's appeal to His very real need, the Son of Man turns to the Word of the heavenly Father. Since fulfilling the Father's will was the entire purpose and meaning of Christ's life, He remains faithful to the Law even in the storm of the harshest physical trials.

Beside these hardships, Christ was forced to face relationship issues worse than ours. Just take a close look at the following situations and imagine yourself under the same circumstances. What would your reaction be and how long would you hold fast in your righteousness?

Pharisees and lawyers constantly seek opportune moments to find fault with Him.

His family believes gossip that He is out of His mind, and they come to take Him home with them.

His disciples are not just slow to learn the principles of the Kingdom of God — they find nothing better to do than to argue about thrones right when Christ confides in them about His coming suffering. He asks them, "Please, keep watch with me," and they fall asleep. He is arrested — and they scatter.

Have you ever had to live through anything like this? How soon did you come to the end of yourself?

Jesus found Himself in dangerous situations — yet he never spoke half-truths. He was slandered, He was spoken of in the most outrageously stupid terms, He was treated like nothing — yet he never lost His temper.

He was a grown man and lived in a body like ours — yet He never gave in to lust.

He had the right to rest — yet He received throngs of people daily with their problems, worries, questions.

Jesus Christ experienced difficulties of the highest degree — yet He was the first and only man to ever remain faithful to the will of the heavenly Father. And it was not because He was incapable of sinning — like a preprogrammed robot. It was because *He could sin, yet He did not.*

There is not one human being in the universe like our Redeemer. This is why this clarification is of such importance: "sending his own Son in the likeness of sinful flesh."

When Christ's life on earth was coming to its end, in a heart-to-heart talk with His disciples He summed things up: "In spite of all of Satan's devices, I never yielded to him, not for a moment." Satan had nothing he could use against Jesus.

> I will no longer talk much with you, for the ruler of this world is coming. **He has no claim on me**. (John 14:30)

That means that Jesus Christ was righteous in every action, in every thought. He actually fulfilled all the requirements of God's law. In Galatians, Paul writes about it in these terms:

> But when the fullness of time had come, God sent forth his Son, **born of woman, born under the law**, to redeem those who were under the law, so that we might receive adoption as sons. (Gal. 4:4–6)

Imputed righteousness

By assuming human flesh and fulfilling God's perfect Law in every situation, Christ laid the foundation for our justification. And now His factual righteous life is imputed to anyone born of Him — the life that God expected of us but that we were unable to present to Him.

> Therefore, as one trespass led to condemnation for all men, so **one act of righteousness leads to justification and life for all men.** (Rom. 5:18)
>
> For God has done what the law, weakened by the flesh, could not do. By sending his own Son in the likeness of sinful flesh and for sin, he condemned sin in the flesh, in order that the righteous requirement of the law might be fulfilled in us, **who walk not according to the flesh but according to the Spirit.** (Rom. 8:3−4)

In Christ the believer has fulfilled the Law. And it is not in just isolated situations that he fulfilled the law — he fulfilled it to the last letter throughout his entire life. The word "πληρόω" ("fulfilled") implies filling up to the brim, a complete filling that leaves nothing to be desired — one more drop and the content will overflow.

Christ fulfilled the Law for us all — and that is grace, that you, a true Christian man or woman, have fulfilled absolutely all of the Law in Christ Jesus. He lived that Law-fulfilling life for you, for me, and for all that belong to Him.

By the very definition of fairness, it is quite difficult to justify what is unjust. In this life people often do it. But that does not alter the objective nature of what is right. It does not change the way God sees it either. Justifying one who is unjust goes against God's very nature.

> He who justifies the wicked and he who condemns the righteous are both alike an abomination to the Lord. (Prov. 17:15)

God cannot simply look the other way and say, "Fine, let's consider him righteous." Only man can be bribed — not God. In God's system of standards, everything is clear, and facts cannot be altered. For a man to become righteous, he needs a real, factual life of righteousness.

> For if while we were enemies we were reconciled to God by the death of his Son, much more, now that we are reconciled, **shall we be saved by his life.** (Rom. 5:10)

The moment we are born again, Jesus' life becomes our life, the factual righteousness of God incarnate becomes our righteousness as a result of an unbreakable union between our spirit and the Spirit of God.

> For God has done what the law, weakened by the flesh, could not do. By sending his own Son in the likeness of sinful flesh and for sin, he condemned sin in the flesh, **in order that the righteous requirement of the law might be fulfilled in us who walk not according to the flesh but according to the Spirit.** (Rom. 8:3–4)

Paul emphasizes this when he says, "In order that the righteous requirement of the law might be fulfilled in us" — and then he adds an important clause: "Who walk not according to the flesh but according to the Spirit." This line brings us to the second principle.

HUNGRY FOR RIGHTEOUSNESS

As we have already noted, many people ask a very reasonable question: If we are saved by Christ's righteousness, if our own righteousness cannot be the basis for justification before God, if it is not only the death of Jesus Christ that is imputed to us but His life as well — why should we even try to live holy lives? Does this approach not give us a license for debauchery?

Paul responds, "By no means!" in an emphatic and unambiguous way, and he presents several valid arguments that explain why this is impossible. One of them is that those who are saved by Christ possess an integral hunger and thirst for righteousness. He discusses this in chapter eight of the book of Romans, immediately after the statement concerning the righteousness of Christ imputed to us.

The following verse starts with the word "For." Here the apostle talks about two categories of people: those living according to the flesh, and those living according to the Spirit. Our task is to determine what sets these people apart.

> For those who live according to the flesh set their minds on the things of the flesh, but those who live according to the Spirit set their minds on the things of the Spirit.
>
> For to set the mind on the flesh is **death**, but to set the mind on the Spirit is life and peace. For the mind that is set on the flesh is **hostile to God, for it does not submit to God's law**; indeed, it cannot. Those who are in the flesh **cannot please God**. (Rom. 8:5–8)

The mind of the flesh is in a state of war against God; it has a value system that is rooted in human conceit, man's urge to self-gratification, and arrogance. It is clear that Paul uses this idea of the fleshly person to identify people who are not born again. Flesh and fleshly interests are the foundation and the center of their world. They want to satisfy their desires, not God's, which ultimately leads them to death.

But believers possess entirely different characteristics. They yearn for that which is of God. They live according to the Spirit, which means that they think according to the value system of the Spirit. God is the center of their worldview. They look at life through a spiritual lens. This is why their life is marked by profound peace.

Several verses later, the apostle says yet again that the life of those born of God is necessarily directed by the Spirit.

> You, however, are not in the flesh but in the Spirit, if in fact the Spirit of God dwells in you. Anyone who does not have the Spirit of Christ does not belong to him. (Rom.8:9)

It is not only the super-spiritual we are talking about. Anyone who belongs to Christ, anyone in whom the Spirit of God lives, will inevitably strive to live according to the Spirit. Striving for righteousness is one of the principal results of the imputed righteousness of Jesus that manifests itself practically. Those who live according to the flesh, in the fleshly value system, are not merely weak believers — they do "not belong to Him." They are not even saved.

Let us make another observation from this passage: Those who have Christ in them also have Christ's attitude toward sin and righteousness. They do not need sin; they live to do God's will just like Jesus lived to do it.

> But if Christ is in you, although the body is dead because of sin, **the Spirit is life because of righteousness.** (Rom. 8:10)

Paul states that being joined with Christ Who is righteous produces in the believer a desire for righteousness too — not merely at the level of wishing, but at the level of the will, expressing itself in practical action.

> For those who **live according to the flesh** set their minds on the things of the flesh, but those who **live according to the Spirit set their minds on the things of the Spirit.** (Rom. 8:5)

Those who receive Christ's righteousness love it and hold it dear. It drives their soul. It is pleasurable. They don't think righteously because they are forced to, but because they want to. There is, however, another kind of people.

> For to set the mind on the flesh is **death**, but to set the mind on the Spirit is life and peace. For the mind that is set on the flesh is **hostile to God, for it does not submit to God's law;** indeed, it cannot. Those who are in the flesh **cannot please God.** (Rom. 8:6–8)

These verses are extremely significant! If you do not rely on the life of Jesus Christ in your salvation, your own "righteousness" will not save you. Those who hope to earn right standing before God by the quality of their life on earth cannot satisfy the standards of God's holiness. They are "hostile to God," no matter how religious they may seem. Why is that?

> For it does not submit to God's law; indeed, it cannot. (Rom. 8:8)

By calling man-centered desires "hostile," the apostle indicates that everything people produce with their own efforts is, in essence, fighting against God. People do not, on their own without the work of the Holy Spirit, want to submit to God. They are absolutely incapable of pleasing Him. Only one Man was ever both willing and able to submit to the Lord in everything, always, and it was the God-Man Jesus Christ.

Only by being "plugged in" to His life do we truly submit to God. In Him we do what God wants from us. In

Galatians, Paul gives us a little different perspective of this truth:

> But when the fullness of time had come, God sent forth his Son, born of woman, born under the law, to redeem those who were under the law, so that we might receive adoption as sons. **And because you are sons, God has sent the Spirit of his Son into our hearts, crying, "Abba! Father!"** (Gal. 4:4–6)

Look at the logic we can glean from this: Christ was "born of woman," which means he was a real man. Christ was "born under the law," which means that he practiced righteousness in real life. And this enabled Him, first, to redeem those who were also under the curse of the Law, and second, to adopt them by the Holy Spirit. As a result of becoming one with Christ, we have become God's children, partakers of His nature, and of His longing for true righteousness.

We have already discussed two aspects. We have mentioned that Christ became man *to make us righteous* and to place in our hearts the very *longing for righteousness*. Thirdly, Christ was born to become *an example of righteousness* for us.

A RIGHTEOUS EXAMPLE

It is reasonable to deduce that Christians should live the way Jesus Christ Himself lived. But here we meet with resistance and counterarguments: "Christ lived two thousand years ago. Today we live in a different culture, under different circumstances..."

People like to create a new, culturally adapted Christ for themselves. Today, the Son of God that people imagine has a variety of faces: faces of actors and the characters they play, faces of politicians and public figures, faces of religious leaders and intellectuals. Truth be told, these social figures are the ones who determine how people live. Anyone but Jesus Christ...

Many claim to be Christians, but how have they come up with the standards of their Christianity? When you say you are a Christian, ask yourself who you consider to be your hero. Whose example do you follow? Who do you imitate? Whose advice has a practical influence on your actions? Who dictates your style, your manners? Do you treat people the way Christ treated them? Do you dress the way He would dress? What do you watch? What do you read? How do you use money? How do you approach any of life's issues? How often does this principle dictate your choices — "to live like Christ"?

Regrettably, many so-called "Christians" wish to act upon their own desires within the "norm" that they themselves set up. However, Christianity is not an individual life model, and not even the model dictated by the majority. God sent His Son Who showed us what being righteous really means.

Jesus Christ demonstrated this many times. What did Jesus say to His disciples when they were consumed with the desire to have the first place?

> But Jesus called them to him and said,
>
> "You know that the rulers of the Gentiles lord it over them, and their great ones exercise authority over them. It shall not be so among you.
>
> But whoever would be great among you must be your servant, and whoever would be first among you must be your slave, even as the Son of Man came not to be served but to serve, and to give his life as a ransom for many." (Matt. 20:25–28)

What was to be their point of reference? *"Do not act the way people act in the world. Rather, live the way I live!"*

Christ's followers preferred — already back then — to live according to their own ideas of what is good and what is bad. And today, there are many believers who talk about Christ and preach Him, yet their lives are not ruled by Him. We only need to look at the arrogant posters of Christian music bands and Christian conferences, and many things will become clear.

But Jesus Christ came to this earth to establish an example of life to follow so that we would not create false Christs when we say that we want to live like Him. He came for us to have a clear picture of Who God really is and of how we should live if we want to imitate Him.

> For to this you have been called, because Christ also suffered for you, **leaving you an example, so that you might follow in his steps.**

> He committed no sin, neither was deceit found in his mouth.
>
> When he was reviled, he did not revile in return; when he suffered, he did not threaten, but continued entrusting himself to him who judges justly. (1 Pet. 2:21–23)

The Scripture says, "leaving you an example" and clarifies: "He committed no sin. He did not flatter. When he was reviled, he did not revile in return. When he suffered, he did not threaten, but trusted God." This is a very practical example!

When Paul chose this example to follow, he rejected all his prior ideals.

> But whatever gain I had, I counted as loss for the sake of Christ. Indeed, I count everything as loss because of the surpassing worth of knowing Christ Jesus my Lord. For his sake I have suffered the loss of all things and count them as rubbish, in order that I may gain Christ. (Phil. 3:7–8)

Following Christ was the biggest passion of Paul's life. That is why all his letters are filled with fervent invitations to imitate the Lord:

> Be imitators of me, as I am of Christ. (1 Cor. 11:1)

For this reason, he asserted that true Christian life is not religious and moral renewal, but is life according to the image and likeness of Christ:

> And we all, with unveiled face, **beholding the glory of the Lord, are being transformed into the same image** from one degree of glory to another. For this comes from the Lord who is the Spirit. (2 Cor. 3:18)

This is what the Christian life is about, friends. Jesus Christ was born, matured, and died so that we could live our lives looking to Him as our example, and so that you and I would have no illusions. It is not merely being kind. It is not just making wise choices. Christianity is a religion of worshipping Christ, a religion of following Christ, a religion of love for Christ.

It's true that for many the life of Jesus Christ is not their day-to-day standard. To be honest, it does not even appeal to them. You hear such people talk about self-liberation, reaching their potential. So I have to ask, could such people even be called Christians? Who does their life belong to — Christ or themselves? His purposes or their dreams? Doesn't it seem bizarre and contradictory that people claiming the name of Christ could have goals and values different from the goals and values of their God and Savior? Such people either don't know Him at all, or they count His opinion as nothing.

I often talk to people who say, "Show me, where does it say that I can't do this?" Wrong approach. Ask a different question: Is it like Christ? When you stream a movie, play a song on your phone, or open a webpage, ask yourself, "Whose standards does this meet?"

"Come on, everyone does this!" isn't enough. Rather, it should be, "Does Jesus do such things? Do His standards and principles allow for this?"

Jesus Christ did not live on this earth just to go down in history. He lived, as Peter puts it, "leaving you an example, so that you might follow in his steps."

Many years ago Charles Sheldon suggested a saying, which was popular again in recent years in American culture: "What would Jesus do?" Yes, I know — it has been used and abused. Yet it is a question that nails it: What would Jesus do? How would He act in my specific situation? That was the very reason Jesus lived on this earth — for us to know the answer to this question for our lives.

Imitating Christ and being transformed into His image are the only reasons worth living. How often do you ask yourself, "What would Christ do in my place?"

In summary, we have already considered these reasons that caused Christ to leave heaven and come to earth as a regular man:

- To make us righteous and justify us by fulfilling the Law in our place.
- To make us long for righteousness by living within us.
- To show an example of righteousness by living a real human life right before our eyes.

And finally…

- Christ lived a human life to bring our righteousness to perfection by becoming our Intercessor.

INTERCESSOR

Living in flesh that is influenced by sin, we remain very weak creatures. And by ourselves, without being assisted and supported by Jesus Christ, we are, plainly speaking, incapable of living. At the end of the eighth chapter of Romans that we have been studying, we find a very interesting verse.

> Who shall bring any charge against God's elect? It is God who justifies.
>
> Who is to condemn? Christ Jesus is the one who died — more than that, who was raised — who is at the right hand of God, **who indeed is interceding for us**. (Rom. 8:33–34)

The apostle revisits something he already mentioned in the first verse. He said in verse one, "There is therefore now no condemnation," and now he reiterates the same thought: "Who shall bring any charge against God's elect? It is God who justifies." But why does God justify them? It is because Christ died, rose again, and is now at the right hand of the Father, *interceding for them*.

Every person that belongs to Him — young or old, spiritually strong or weak — having been written on the palms of Jesus Christ, is on His mind and in His heart.

And every time a true Christian gets weary, stumbles, or even falls, the Lord Jesus addresses His Heavenly Father and intercedes for him or her.

There is another reason why the intercession of the Son of God is important for us — because the devil is doing exactly the opposite. Every time one of us stumbles, he comes to God and says, "Look, he fell. Again!" Satan is a malicious accuser. Listen to what is said about him.

> And the great dragon was thrown down, that ancient serpent, who is called the devil and Satan, the deceiver of the whole world — he was thrown down to the earth, and his angels were thrown down with him.
>
> And I heard a loud voice in heaven, saying, "Now the salvation and the power and the kingdom of our God and the authority of his Christ have come, for the **accuser** of our brothers has been thrown down, **who accuses them day and night before our God.**" (Rev. 12:9–10)

It is a horrible picture: You stumble — he records it. You grow weak — he exposes it. You waiver — he trumpets this fact for all the citizens of heaven to hear! This is Satan's job, and it is critical for our Representative in heaven to advocate for us, weak humans, before the heavenly Father. This cannot be done by the virgin Mary, or by the saints of all the ages, or by your family members. He alone can do it. And there are several reasons for this.

Living righteously in the flesh

Christ has the right to do intercede for us. He has lived righteously as a man. And He imputes His righteousness to us.

> My little children, I am writing these things to you so that you may not sin. But if anyone does sin, **we have an advocate with the Father, Jesus Christ the righteous. He is the propitiation for our sins**, and not for ours only but also for the sins of the whole world. (1 John 2:1–2)

So, we have to be absolutely sure that we are in Him. If you are not in Christ, your name is not mentioned in heaven! For this very reason we encourage each other to examine ourselves constantly to know whether we are true believers!

It does not matter whether the church accepted you as a member, whether they baptized you, or whether they called you to join in a ministry. Pastors can be deceived. But it is a true tragedy when a person is in the church, yet not in Christ — when his or her name is on the church roll, but not mentioned before the throne in heaven. This is why I ask the question, "Was there a moment when your status changed from 'not in Him' to 'in Him'?"

In Ephesians Paul clarifies who exactly is found "in Him":

> In him you also, when you heard the word of truth, the gospel of your salvation, and believed in him, were sealed with the promised Holy Spirit. (Eph. 1:13)

When were these people placed in Christ? The moment they were born, baptized, prayed over by ministers? No, it was the moment they heard the Word of truth and believed in Him — it was then and only then that they were sealed with the Holy Spirit. The righteousness of Jesus Christ was imputed to them by faith, and today they have an Advocate.

Suffering in the flesh

You've heard people complain that no one can empathize with them. "My situation is unique," they say. But it is not so with Christ. He is fully aware of the burden, hardship, pain, and suffering you and I experience here on earth.

I have met people who, when traveling from a developed country to a less developed one, have brought medicine, drinking water, and even chocolate with them. Jesus, on the contrary, left all the heavenly riches behind when He became a man. He was real, simple, authentic. He experienced all the pain. And when you hurt, He knows what it is like. He knows how it feels to be betrayed, to be persecuted. This is why He is able to be an intercessor: He is capable of comprehending and feeling with you.

> Therefore, he **had to be made like his brothers in every respect**, so that he might become a merciful and faithful high priest in the service of God, to make propitiation for the sins of the people.
>
> **For because he himself has suffered when tempted, he is able to help those who are being tempted.** (Heb. 2:17–18)

The book of Hebrews continues:

> For we do not have a high priest who is **unable to sympathize with our weaknesses**, but one who in every respect **has been tempted as we are, yet without sin**.
>
> Let us then with confidence draw near to the throne of grace, that we may receive mercy and find grace to help in time of need. (Heb. 4:15–16)

Jesus has experienced it all. When you go through trials, remember that Jesus has already walked this journey. He has been in your shoes. Christ's life is the driving force behind His compassionate intercession.

The truth of the value of the life of Jesus Christ is as complex as the mystery of divine incarnation itself. Understanding it is crucially important for us to live a joy-filled Christian life, for us to have a profound appreciation of what Christ accomplished, for us to have a point of reference in our daily struggles against sin, and for us to come boldly to God's throne in the most difficult and most glorious moments of our lives.

WHAT DO *YOU* THINK OF CHRIST?

- First of all, examine yourself to see if you are joined with Christ not only in His death but also in His life. If you are not sure, please do not linger on this issue. Give yourself over to God today.

- If you are a believer, what practical actions do you take every day to live that day the way Christ would have?

- Examine yourself: Is the life of Jesus Christ really the standard for your life? Do you love Him so much that you will "count everything as rubbish" and align your life with the desires and sentiments of Jesus Christ?

CHAPTER IV
BORN TO RISE FROM THE DEAD

For as by a man came death,
by a man has come also the
resurrection of the dead. | 1 Cor. 15:21

Due to its volume, one New Testament epistle stands out among all written by Paul — 1 Corinthians. Chapter 15 dominates with 58 verses. Surprisingly, almost the entire chapter argues for our Lord's physical resurrection.

The reason for this lengthy discussion of the resurrection is that by the time of the writing of this epistle, certain people had appeared in Corinth who claimed that Christianity does not necessarily include a belief in the resurrection of the body. They taught that after death people turn into bodiless spirits, and in that state they abide in heaven. Realizing that this heresy distorts the entire story of salvation, Paul treated it with utmost seriousness.

> Now I would remind you, brothers, of the gospel I preached to you, which you received, in which you stand, and by which you are being saved, if you hold fast to the word I preached to you — unless you believed in vain.
>
> For I delivered to you as of first importance what I also received: that Christ died for our sins in accordance with the Scriptures, hat he was buried, that **he was raised on the third day in accordance with the Scriptures.** (1 Cor. 15:1–4)

The apostle dwells on the key elements of the Gospel: Christ died, was buried[6] and "was raised on the third day in accordance with the Scriptures." In other words, since the resurrection is included as a critical component of the Gospel, if we eliminate it, we lose a very important element of the message of salvation.

The truth of Christ's resurrection was not important to Paul alone. It played a significant part in the message of the apostles in general. Virtually every sermon by the apostles mentioned in the New Testament makes a reference to the resurrection. And it is not merely referenced — it is a governing theme in these messages.

Remember the very first sermon spoken on the day of Pentecost:

---

[6] In this case, burial acts as proof of death.

> This Jesus, delivered up according to the definite plan and foreknowledge of God, you crucified and killed by the hands of lawless men. **God raised him up**, losing the pangs of death, because it was not possible for him to be held by it. (Acts 2:23–24)

The statement concerning resurrection is a kind of climax in Peter's sermon. Its principal argument is as follows: *Christ is the Messiah because He overcame death.*

Just in this sermon, the resurrection is mentioned three times. All in all, the book of Acts makes over twenty references to the truth of the Messiah's return to life. It is also interesting that the author often uses the word "resurrection" as a synonym for the word "Gospel."

> And with great power the apostles were giving their **testimony to the resurrection of the Lord Jesus**, and great grace was upon them all. (Acts 4:33)

It may be difficult to resist the question, "Were there not enough other facts in the life of Jesus Christ worth preaching about? Why did the apostles keep coming back to this particular event? Is the truth of Jesus Christ's physical resurrection that important for our salvation?"

Throughout this book, we have been making an effort to answer the question of why Christ assumed a physical body. One of the reasons for that was a necessity for the Messiah to be raised up in the flesh. And soon we will discover the very reason why it was crucial.

When speaking of various doctrines, we often get so used to them that we rarely give them much thought. Christ is risen — we think, "So what? Black and white. What else is there to understand?" But in thinking this way, we skim the surface and overlook a huge number of blessings hidden in the facts told us in the Gospels.

Consider this question: "If before His incarnation the Messiah did not have a body, then upon dying He could simply go back to the Father in His spirit… Why would He then need to come back into a body?" Because at the time of His death, Jesus committed His spirit to His Father.

> Then Jesus, calling out with a loud voice, said, "**Father, into your hands I commit my spirit!**" And having said this he breathed his last. (Luke 23:46)

The birth of Jesus Christ is the moment of divine incarnation, implying that there was a time when Christ as the God-Man did not exist. He has always existed as God, but the Son of God became the God-Man at a very specific moment in history. It happened at the moment of conception, performed supernaturally by the Holy Spirit. The angel announced the imminent birth of Christ to Mary in this way:

> And the angel answered her, "The Holy Spirit will come upon you, and the power of the Most High will overshadow you; therefore the child to be born will be called holy — the Son of God." (Luke 1:35)

This means that Jesus Christ came in the Spirit and assumed flesh. Then in the Spirit He departed earth and joined the Father. This begs the question, "Why did He need to come back to the cold tomb? Why did He need this battered body? Why rise from the dead? Why continue to be confined in human flesh? Couldn't He depart the same way He came?"

These are all valid questions that go deep into the mystery of the divine incarnation.

> Great indeed, we confess, is the mystery of godliness: He was manifested in the flesh. (1 Tim. 3:16)

Researching this topic not only helps us grasp the importance of Christ coming to this earth, but also helps us appreciate God's precious gift manifested in the incarnate Son of God. It gives us a solid foundation in life that has been established by Jesus Christ.

| CHRIST'S TRIUMPH OVER DEATH AND CORRUPTION |

Every one of us, in spite of all the joys of this life, has to deal with one unshakeable and sad reality: corruption and death. Every living organism eventually dies. Multiple studies have shown that from the moment of our birth our cells begin to die, and this is a never-ending and accelerating process.

We live in corruption. We head for death. We get sick. Our bodies grow weak and degenerate. We lose our attractiveness. The brain begins to forget. Broken bones do not heal well. Once we get ill, it gets difficult to recover. It is a terrible phenomenon!

We are plagued by this and we get used to it. We attempt to navigate between these inevitable facts of corruption as if dodging holes in a road, hoping to somehow make it through, to live on. But whether we like it or not, we will all have to die someday. And few people ponder how wrong this is! A rosy-cheeked baby turns into a wrinkled wretch in a matter of seventy years? — Why?!

Corruption is the facet of our existence where the destructive consequences of sin are most obvious. It eats away at our bodies, saps our strength, and ultimately succeeds at complete and utter destruction. This is why the salvation of mankind not only calls for the forgiveness of sins and propitiation for our guilt, but also calls for a victory over the irreversible consequences of sin — namely, corruption and death.

THE PROBLEM OF CORRUPTION

God created man to have both a spirit and a body.

> Then the Lord God formed the man of dust from the ground and breathed into his nostrils the breath of life, and the man became a living creature. (Gen. 2:7)

The human body was formed out of God-created matter — the physical elements of the earth's crust. This is one of the main differences between humans and angels. Having no bodies, they are largely immune to our problems. Of course, they do not experience the joys of living in the body either. But man was created to be an entirely new and different being.

First, he was created as a person carrying the image and the likeness of God. But, on top of that, he was created as a person in a body, which means that his soul, his internal component, is intimately connected with his physical being.

When man sinned, as a consequence, sin affected not only his spiritual being but his physical one too. Sin entered the material world on the genetic level. So even if you place man in the safest, most bacteria-free and virus-free place on earth, nullifying any threat to his life, he will one day still die on his own. The genes of death will eventually set in motion irreversible chemical processes — and he will give in. And he is not alone. As a result of man's actions, the entire world is dying a slow death.

Man's life is directly linked to the earth. After sin, God caused the earth to suffer the curse as well, and it affected all creation. This is why leaves fall, animals die, soil is eroded, and weeds stifle agricultural plans.

> And to Adam he said, "Because you have listened to the voice of your wife and have eaten of the tree of which I commanded you, 'You shall not eat of it,' **cursed is the ground because of you**; in pain

> you shall eat of it all the days of your life; thorns and thistles it shall bring forth for you; and you shall eat the plants of the field.
>
> By the sweat of your face you shall eat bread, till you return to the ground, for out of it you were taken; for you are dust, and to dust you shall return." (Gen. 3:17—19)

Man, like the entire animal and plant world, does not have life in himself. He was not created for independent existence. We cannot live without a connection with God[7]. The Scripture says that God literally holds together the elementary particles of the physical world.

> For by him all things were created, in heaven and on earth, visible and invisible, whether thrones or dominions or rulers or authorities — all things were created through him and for him. And he is before all things, and **in him all things hold together.** (Col. 1:16—17)

Sin disrupted the life-giving connection between man and God. As soon as man was disconnected from the Source of his life, he immediately started dying. He has a small life resource (similar to a computer that can run for some time on battery power), but it is very limited, and man disintegrates irreversibly.

In his book *Cancer Ward*, A.I. Solzhenitsyn described life in the oncology department — real life stories, real people. The story tells the profound tragedy of what wicked people go through as they face the ruthless reality of death.

---

[7] Heb. 1:3; 2 Pet. 3:7; Rom. 11:36.

Each of the people depicted had thrilling lives: They all had dreams, plans, and faith in a bright future. But suddenly, the doctor announced, "This is it. There is no more life" — and they hit a wall. All at once, they came to their senses. In an instant, they realized that time was short. And in the blink of an eye, all they had lived for lost its luster.

Solzhenitsyn brilliantly conveyed the atmosphere of dismay and hopelessness reigning in this hospital cancer ward hospital where man comes to a profound realization of his own powerlessness. He is staring death in the face — something beyond his control, something much stronger than him, something that does not ask his opinion of when he should leave this earth. All of a sudden, each one sees that he is affected by hideous and murderous corruption — and that there is nothing he can do to resist it.

Death is a ruthless reality that tramples human dreams.

Solzhenitsyn wrote this book to show that we are all patients in a huge "cancer ward." No one recovers here. No one is discharged.

Remember the moment when you stood by a coffin, looking at the stiff, lifeless body of someone dear to you. This sight is often more than we can bear, and we are filled with an overwhelming sense of horror and despair. The person who just a few days ago lived, thought, talked, had feelings, dreams, aspirations… is now decaying. While still alive, this person was appreciated, desired, loved… As soon as he or she turned into a corpse, all people want to do is get rid of the body. Sin has distorted the physical world.

But this situation becomes even more unbearable when one realizes that death puts a decisive end to everyone's life. The fact that this is universal is of no comfort. On the contrary, you have an abrupt, vivid realization that no economic resources, no intellectual advantage, no high social status will help you at this checkpoint. Inevitably, man returns to dust according to the punishment pronounced by God. Peter refers to people as "slaves of corruption."

> They promise them freedom, but they themselves are slaves of corruption. (2 Pet. 2:19)

This is a very accurate description of humanity. Some people think that their billions will give them freedom. Others rely on change through political means or look to a scientific breakthrough. But in this passage, speaking about false teachers, Peter emphasizes that trust in people — in any person — makes no sense. No billionaires, political figures, philosophers or religious gurus — no one is able to solve the problem of death because they too are its slaves. It epitomizes the powerlessness of humanity.

Mankind did not just need a minor fix. People needed to be brought back to life. So, Christ had to come in the flesh to solve this problem in the most profound way.

Jesus Christ is the only One Who can claim authority over death because He Himself is free of corruption and death. In Him there is life.

> For the wages of sin is death, but the free gift of God is **eternal life in Christ Jesus our Lord** (Rom. 6:23)

Death is the most obvious problem in the world. Global warming, world hunger, fuel shortages — all that comes far behind the problem of physical corruption. Of course, we have to deal with the issue of spiritual corruption, but it is not as obvious externally. However, when people grow old, get sick, and die, then everyone admits the power of sin.

VICTORY OVER CORRUPTION

The story of God's victory over corruption is amazing, and it is a vivid demonstration of the riches of His heart and mind. God stood on the same level with mankind, experienced the effect of death, overcame it, and then freed from corruption all who are in Christ.

> Since therefore the children share in flesh and blood, he himself likewise partook of the same things, that through death he might destroy the one who has the power of death, that is, the devil, and deliver all those who through fear of death were subject to lifelong slavery. (Heb. 2:14–15)

The Son of God had to "partake" of flesh and blood — he had to become forever a full-blooded man, a legitimate representative of mankind. He did not just have to take upon Himself the sin of humanity and carry the punishment for it. He had to die so that once risen from the dead, He could bring us also out of the death chamber.

This is a very important factor. We read in the Scripture that at times angels appeared in physical form. It seems logical to deduce that to carry out some of God's assignments, spiritual beings are able to temporarily assume human flesh or at least appear as a human.

But the incarnation of the Son was no mere temporary assumption of human appearance, nor an actor playing a part. It was God's eternal unification with the human race. That is why, unlike fleshless angels, the God-Man could die.

The power of resurrection

The Scripture emphasizes that this victory could only be achieved by colossal, superhuman power. Death could not hold Jesus Christ, even though it clung to Him with all of its tentacles.

> This Jesus, delivered up according to the definite plan and foreknowledge of God, you crucified and killed by the hands of lawless men. God raised him up, loosing the pangs of death, **because it was not possible for him to be held by it.** (Acts 2:23–24)

The source of this power is God Himself.

> I do not cease to give thanks for you, remembering you in my prayers…that you may know what is the hope to which he has called you, what are the riches of his glorious inheritance in the saints, and what is the immeasurable greatness of his power toward us who believe, **according to the working of his great**

> **might that he worked in Christ when he raised him from the dead** and seated him at his right hand in the heavenly places. (Eph. 1:16, 18–20)

Only God possesses the kind of power that can bring the dead to life, and nothing can compare to it.

Having become the God-Man, Christ continued as the Source of life. He did not lose His divine nature and power. Besides, He did not just come to this earth as a righteous person. He lived a human life *without committing the slightest sin.* This is why death could not hold Him.

Have you seen springs of water coming from the ground? If you try to put a small sandhill on top of the mouth of the spring, in a matter of seconds the fountain will break through and surface. Why? Because a spring has a *power.* It's not a puddle.

But what would happen if several tons of sand were dumped on the spring? Would water still find its way to the surface? The answer to this question will depend on the strength of the source.

Human sin weighed upon Jesus Christ as the heaviest burden possible. The weight of this sin was so serious that it even paralyzed His physical life for a short time. Hell, death, corruption, and all the sins of humanity came crashing down on the Son of God on the cross of Calvary. They killed His body, but they could not keep Him dead. The God-Man's divine nature, like a powerful fountain, found its way back to life. God's power is much stronger than the power of death, and for this reason, we proclaim triumphantly,

> "O death, where is your victory? O death, where is your sting?" (1 Cor. 15:55)

We find proof of the fact that Jesus is the Source of life for all who trust in Him in the words of Christ Himself spoken during his earthly ministry.

> Jesus said to her, "I am the resurrection and the life. Whoever believes in me, though he die, yet shall he live. (John 11:25)

The magnitude of Christ's resurrection is beyond our mental capacities. It is, without question, one of the most powerful manifestations of God's glorious Person.

The body of the Risen One

The moment Jesus Christ died He committed His spirit to His Heavenly Father. But at His resurrection, the spirit of the Son of God returned into His body. However, something happened to the body!

Christ was still recognizable. The body still retained the marks from the nails and the spear which Christ showed to Thomas[8]. Jesus could talk, eat, walk. But this was an entirely different body! It had new properties. Christ could instantly move through space (Luke 24:31). He could ap-

---

[8] John 20:27.

pear and disappear (Acts 1:3) and walk through physical barriers (John 20:19). And it was in this body that He ascended to His Father (Luke 24:51).

So, by rising from the dead, Jesus Christ did not merely give His torn body a second chance. Resurrection performed a radical transformation of His physical being, making it incorruptible. This is the kind of body that is discussed in 1 Corinthians 15 where Paul explains the details of this amazing phenomenon.

> So is it with the resurrection of the dead. What is sown is perishable; what is raised is imperishable. It is sown in dishonor; it is raised in glory. It is sown in weakness; it is raised in power. (1 Cor. 15:42–43)

The deadly poison — that magnet of death that irresistibly pulls man to the grave — was removed from the cells in His body. Christ's resurrection was different from the resurrection of Lazarus, Tabitha, and others brought back to life: They each came back to an old body which continued getting ill, continued in its corruption, and eventually died a second time. They didn't overcome death — death was merely delayed by a few decades.

Jesus Christ was the first and only Man Who returned into a different and incorruptible body. He did not turn into an angel. He did not merely appear in spirit. He was resurrected into a real body, yet a body that was drastically different from yours and mine. This is why it was said of Him:

> But in fact Christ has been raised from the dead, the firstfruits of those who have fallen asleep. (1 Cor. 15:20)

Just like Christ became the only Man Who never sinned, He was also the only Man Who rose from the dead never to die again. His body does not feel death anymore. His body is not prone to aging. It doesn't need medication. Christ's body is beyond the power of death. Being the very Source of life, Christ broke through the layers of sin and death.

In this respect, the body of the risen Christ is different from the bodies of Adam and Eve before the fall. It is a glorified body transformed into a different state.

I believe that the truth of Christ's victory over corruption should be the object of our greatest gratitude. Every time your lower back gives you trouble, you have a toothache, your eyesight grows dimmer, you see new wrinkles, gray hair, scars — every time you see signs of corruption in your own body, remember this: Thanks to Jesus Christ coming in the flesh, thanks to Him dying in your place and rising from the dead, a new body is awaiting you — without wrinkles or extra weight, a body that will never need wheelchairs or crutches. This is the miracle of resurrection — the resurrection of the God-Man in the flesh!

| OUR FREEDOM FROM CORRUPTION |

Even if Christ's resurrection was only for His benefit, it would be a miracle worthy of our attention. But the true magnitude of this event is that Jesus not only broke free from captivity to death Himself — He also freed us — humanity!

> But in fact Christ has been raised from the dead, **the firstfruits of those who have fallen asleep.** (1 Cor. 15:20)

Christ did not do this just for His sake, nor just to prove that the issue of death can, in fact, be solved. Neither was it to demonstrate His astonishing power and inconceivable wisdom. He did it to convince us that *we will be raised again like Him.*

Of course, mortals have a hard time believing in resurrection. We are so used to corruption that it's hard to seriously entertain the possibility of immortality. This is why the wise men of Athens listened to Paul only to the point when he began preaching of resurrection. Listening to such words was beneath their intellectual dignity.

> Now when they heard of the resurrection of the dead, some mocked. But others said, "We will hear you again about this." (Acts 17:32)

The Corinthians also had serious difficulties believing in the resurrection of the dead. They are strikingly similar to today's liberal Christians who believe that Christianity is only good for helping us live this earthly life. But resurrection is real, and the holy Scriptures explain how we can rely on this truth and boldly build our lives on this foundation.

A CONDITION OF DELIVERANCE

As was already mentioned, the message to the church in Corinth contains a detailed explanation of why the resurrection of believers is conditioned upon the resurrection of the Lord Jesus Christ.

> But in fact Christ has been raised from the dead, **the firstfruits of those who have fallen asleep.** For as by a man came death, by a man has come also the resurrection of the dead. For as in Adam all die, **so also in Christ shall all be made alive.** But each in his own order: **Christ the firstfruits, then at his coming those who belong to Christ.** (1 Cor. 15:20–23)

The apostle demonstrates that the future physical resurrection of believers is conditioned on two factors: the resurrection of Jesus Christ Himself and our unbreakable union with Him.

Paul emphasizes again Christ's human nature: "For as by a man came death, by a man has come also the resurrection of the dead." Then, he gives a clear comparison: "For as in Adam all die, so also in Christ shall all be made alive." Just as death is real and unescapable for all the descendants of Adam, resurrection is real and unescapable for all who are Christ's, all who have been redeemed by Him, all who have God's Spirit dwelling in them, all who possess His nature. In other words, those who are in Christ cannot help but come alive again!

In His sermons, Christ repeatedly emphasized that His life in a believer cannot be consumed by death — period.

John 6 describes a situation where Jesus fed several thousand. It is not surprising that the next day the people went looking for Christ again, hoping the miracle would happen again. But right when they finally found Him, Christ announced that they were seeking the wrong thing.

> Do not work for the food that perishes, but for the food that endures to eternal life, which the Son of Man will give to you. For on him God the Father has set his seal. (John 6:27)

These people had made a long journey — crossing over to one side of the lake, then to the other. They had invested so much time and effort. Why? Just to receive one more serving of bread and fish. They sought perishable food that could only support life for a short time in their fading bodies. But Christ warned them, "Invest in what will give you eternal life." What is this true, non-perishable food?

> So Jesus said to them, "Truly, truly, I say to you, unless you eat the flesh of the Son of Man and drink his blood, you have no life in you. Whoever feeds on my flesh and drinks my blood has eternal life, and I will raise him up on the last day." (John 6:53–54)

"Do you want to have life? Then you need to feed only on Me. I — and only I — have non-perishable life in Myself." Because we are united with Christ, we need to learn to feed on Christ and live through Him:

> Whoever feeds on my flesh and drinks my blood abides in me, and I in him. As the living Father sent me, and **I live because of the Father, so whoever feeds on me, he also will live because of me.** (John 6:56–57)

What happens is an intimate union between the believer and Christ, comparable to the permanent connection between Christ and God the Father.

> For this is the will of my Father, that everyone who looks on the Son and **believes in him should have eternal life, and I will raise him up on the last day.**" (John 6:40)

Some believe, however, that this passage talks about the ordinance of the Lord's Table. Yes, the bread and the wine symbolize the body and blood of our Lord, but they are not actual, physical body and blood. If you subject them to chemical analysis, it will become obvious that these are perishable food. We observe this ordinance "in remembrance." No matter how much you eat, these elements won't help you overcome corruption and death. That is not the point of the Lord's Table. Its purpose is only to point in the direction of the redemption accomplished by Christ. But this passage talks about the true life we have in Christ. We need to feed on the Lord just like we feed on bread.

Being unified with Him by faith, we have in us His life, a source that cannot be stopped up by any means. This is why the resurrection of Jesus Christ is the basis for our individual victory over corruption.

SOURCE OF LIFE

The reason for both Christ's resurrection and ours is the same. Christ died, but God raised Him from the dead. Why? Because in Him was the source of life — He was God. Every one of us will die, but if God's living Spirit dwells in us, He will raise us up also.

> If the Spirit of him who raised Jesus from the dead dwells in you, he who raised Christ Jesus [a] from the dead will also give life to your mortal bodies through **his Spirit who dwells in you.** (Rom. 8:11)

The last phrase is very important: He will give life to the dead not through the Spirit acting from the outside, but through the Spirit who dwells in them. Do you see how crucial this is? Those who do not have the Spirit of God in them will remain in the ground. They will remain under the power of death.

I will admit, it is beyond me why so many people settle for halfhearted Christianity. They are okay with merely going to church, helping out in this or that ministry, listening to sermons. But this is not enough! It is not enough just to be a good person. Not enough to pray and read the Bible. Not enough to participate in church activities. Not enough to sing Christian songs. Not enough to avoid grave sins. Does this good person have the Spirit of God inside that will raise him or her from the dead? If not, this person is lost! Forever! If someone is not born by the Spirit of God, this person will not rise from the dead! This person's hope and trust are then in vain!

Today, out of fear of appearing backward, many pastors claim that salvation may be obtained without receiving Jesus Christ as Lord of one's life and as one's personal Savior. According to recent surveys in the United States[9], over 50% of those who profess to have been born again share this belief. So, what will happen to all the billions who have never heard the Gospel? What about those born in Muslim countries? What about those who have believed a little but not completely, or have believed but in a somewhat different way? What about those who have performed many kind deeds and great spiritual accomplishments? The answer given by Christ is crystal clear:

> Jesus answered, "Truly, truly, I say to you, **unless one is born of water and the Spirit, he cannot enter the kingdom of God.** That which is born of the flesh is flesh, and that which is born of the Spirit is spirit. (John 3:5–6)

We send no one to hell. All we do is state — on the basis of the Scriptures — that only those who are born of the Spirit of God will be raised from the dead.

Do you know how an object drowned in the sea is raised to the surface? One of the methods is for divers to tie pontoons to the object, and then inflate it with air, and the air floats it up to the top. A similar effect will take place with the resurrection of believers' bodies. If

---

[9] Barna Group (2011, April 18). What Americans Believe About Universalism and Pluralism. Retrieved from www.barna.com: https://www.barna.com/research/what-americans-believe-about-universalism-and-pluralism/#.UkN7FD8myYM

someone has the Spirit of God dwelling inside, then the moment will come when his or her body, buried in the ground, will be raised from the dust. Only God is able to raise from the dead, and for this to happen, it is essential that His Spirit become a part of our nature.

RECEIVING FREEDOM

How can we be certain that we have truly overcome corruption even though we still experience its effects?

Throughout our lives on earth, believers actually don't look any different physically from unbelievers. The only difference may be that some believers are more likely to maintain a healthy lifestyle. Some try to claim that God's children should never be sick, quoting Isaiah 53:4[10]. But that does not work. Even the most zealous preachers of the "prosperity gospel" continue getting sick, growing old, and dying. Where is the victory then?

Deliverance of the spirit

Victory over death is seen, first of all, in the redemption of our spirit and its deliverance from the power of sin. When Paul prayed that God would help Ephesian believers to grasp God's power shown in Christ's resurrection, Paul asked that they would comprehend that they have been raised from the dead by God to a living hope.

---

[10] Surely he has borne our griefs and carried our sorrows; yet we esteemed him stricken, smitten by God, and afflicted. But he was pierced for our transgressions; he was crushed for our iniquities; upon him was the chastisement that brought us peace, and with his wounds we are healed. (Isa. 53:4-5)

> ...even when we were dead in our trespasses, made us alive together with Christ — by grace **you** have been saved — and raised us up with him and seated us with him in the heavenly places in Christ Jesus. (Eph. 2:5–6)

Our resurrection begins with the resurrection of the *spirit*. We are dead in our trespasses and sins; we want to do evil; we are under submission to Satan; we are rebels by nature, the "children of wrath." But the moment we are born again, our *spirit* is resurrected with Christ.

> For you did not receive the spirit of slavery to fall back into fear, but you have received the Spirit of adoption as sons, by whom we cry, "Abba! Father!"
>
> The Spirit himself bears witness with our spirit that we are children of God, and **if children, then heirs — heirs of God and fellow heirs with Christ, provided we suffer with him in order that we may also be glorified with him.** (Rom. 8:15–17)

This passage contains several important truths at once. First, Paul says that being born again is proof of our eternal salvation. As a result of receiving God's Spirit, we begin to have a sincere desire for God as our Father; this is why we cry out to Him, "Abba, Father!" But notice that the apostle continues to develop this idea even further: "And if children, then heirs." If we are children of God, then we have the right to an inheritance just like Jesus Christ does. But Paul drops a caveat: "provided we suffer with Him."

Following Christ is inevitably linked to all sorts of pressure. Just like Jesus Christ suffered in the flesh — fatigue, hunger, thirst and pain — all the while remaining faithful to the Father, God's children will experience something similar.

When we know internally that we belong to God the Father, we have assurance that one day our physical bodies will be freed from corruption:

> ...knowing that he who raised the Lord Jesus will raise us also with Jesus and bring us with you into his presence.... So we do not lose heart. Though our outer self is wasting away, our inner self is being renewed day by day. (2 Cor. 4:14, 16)

The redemption of the spirit is a pledge of the eventual redemption of the body.

Deliverance of the body

Everyone yearns to be free from corruption. No one wants to settle for disease. Everyone wants to triumph over death. Yet only those born of God's Spirit may say with certainty that one day they will receive this freedom:

> For we know that the whole creation has been groaning together in the pains of childbirth until now. And not only the creation, but we ourselves, who have the firstfruits of the Spirit, groan inwardly as we **wait eagerly for adoption as sons, the redemption of our bodies.** (Rom. 8:22–23)

The Holy Spirit who dwells in us justifies this waiting.

In the foundational 1 Corinthians chapter on resurrection, Paul anticipates the way this will happen.

> Behold! I tell you a mystery. **We shall not all sleep, but we shall all be changed**, in a moment, in the twinkling of an eye, at the last trumpet. For the trumpet will sound, and **the dead will be raised imperishable**, and we shall be changed. For this perishable body must put on the imperishable, and this mortal body must put on immortality.
>
> When the perishable puts on the imperishable, and the mortal puts on immortality, then shall come to pass the saying that is written:
>
> "Death is swallowed up in victory."
> "O death, where is your victory?
>   O death, where is your sting?"
> (1 Cor. 15:51–55)

The Scripture promises us that all God's children, both living and dead, will receive new, imperishable bodies similar to that of the risen Messiah, at the moment of His second coming. This is our deliverance and our hope!

> Just as we have borne the image of the man of dust, we shall also bear the image of the man of heaven.
> (1 Cor. 15:49)

In summary, Jesus Christ was born to rise from the dead — and to raise all who are born of Him.

But there is yet another reason why Christ needed to rise in His physical body: His physical resurrection is proof of the legitimacy of our salvation.

| ASSURANCE OF SALVATION |

When the Paul encountered people who claimed to be Christians yet denied the fact of physical resurrection, including the resurrection of Christ, he immediately responded with several sobering objections:

> If Christ has not been raised, your faith is futile and you are still in your sins. Then those also who have fallen asleep in Christ have perished. If in Christ we have hope in this life only, we are of all people most to be pitied. (1 Cor. 15:17–19)

Paul uses two arguments in this passage. He says first that if we assume that Christ did not rise from the dead, then salvation is impossible. And also, without future resurrection, the Christian life is meaningless. We will briefly cover each of these arguments.

No resurrection — no salvation

The physical resurrection of Christ testifies to several important things. First, it was the ultimate proof that Jesus is God.

If the doctrine of Christ were accepted by the entire world, but we lacked this most important proof of His divinity, we could not be certain that He is God. His triumph over death demonstrated that Jesus' claims to be the Messiah are not empty. He did possess an authentic, divine nature, and He did have the source of life in Himself — the source that only God could have.

> And if Christ has not been raised, your faith is futile and **you are still in your sins**. (1 Cor. 15:17)

Without Christ's resurrection, our faith is vain. Paul says that without it, "You are still in your sins." Christ's resurrection was proof that the vicarious sacrifice of the God-Man was accepted, the Father's justice was satisfied, and His wrath was abated. But if Christ was not raised from the dead, then salvation is merely an illusion. We believe, we go to church, we pray, we read our Bibles, we keep the commandments, we do good works — but our sins would still be there.

Faith by itself does not save. The power is in the object of our faith, in the One in Whom we put our trust. This is why we talk of the powerlessness of other religions. They do not have Christ.

> That is why his faith was "counted to him as righteousness." ... It will be counted to us who believe in him who raised from the dead Jesus our Lord, who was delivered up for our trespasses and **raised for our justification**. (Rom. 4:22, 24–25)

The point of the Christian life

Throughout history there have always been people who hold Christian morality in high esteem, but who are utterly unwilling to acknowledge Christ as God or to state that He did, in fact, rise from the dead in a physical body.

Many people have praised the Bible: "It is so on point! How true that we need to live honestly! It has such truth for our society today!" But Paul calls these people, seemingly loyal to Christianity, the most unfortunate people in the world:

> And if Christ has not been raised, your faith is futile and you are still in your sins. Then those also who have fallen asleep in Christ have perished. **If in Christ we have hope in this life only, we are of all people most to be pitied.**

What is sad about these people?

Imagine that you are terminally ill, and you have but a few days left to live. With great difficulty, you manage to obtain medicine that can cure you. The medicine is wrapped beautifully and carries a catchy name. Names of famous researchers adorn the box. The product looks striking. But you choose to put the medicine on the shelf. It looks so good and makes the room so much brighter! It boosts your image with so many well-known names to back it up! You look at it and are happy, but yet you've never used it as intended. What could we say? You are the most unfortunate person in this world: You have the medicine, yet you are still dying!

That is exactly Paul's point. While Christ came to deliver man from sin and death, to give him the chance to spend eternity with God, people want Him instead to give them the ordinary "perishable bread" — a stable society, a strong family, material blessings. If you only need Christ in order to live this earthly life well, one can only feel sorry for you.

It is true that even unbelievers who take Christ's life principles seriously may have a certain advantage in life. If they learn to keep their irritation in check, they will enjoy better physical health and emotional stability. If they control their desires, they will have better financial stability. But the person who uses Christ's principles only to experience success in this life yet ignores the eternal value of Christianity deserves to be pitied. Christ came to give so much more!

If there is no resurrection, then it makes no sense to curb the desires of our flesh and we should enjoy this life to the fullest. If there is no resurrection, Christian morality is not only useless, but it actually goes against logic to deprive yourself of the sinful pleasures of this life. There would be no point. And if this is so, then Christians are truly the "most to be pitied."

But if resurrection is real, it changes everything in the most radical way — both for those who deny Christ and for those who selectively use certain principles of His doctrine. People who do not believe Christ have a problem which cannot be solved by their external adherence to morals, and they risk losing their very souls.

As we close this chapter, I would like to emphasize the following: Christ's physical resurrection is not only one of the greatest miracles in the universe, but also one of the most crucial elements of God's plan of redemption and of the church in general. It demonstrates God's immense power that abides in its fullness in the God-Man Jesus Christ. It gives believers a firm foundation for their faith in the ultimate triumph over corruption in their bodies thanks to the union of their spirit with the life-giving Spirit of God. And finally, Christ's resurrection convinces us that the propitiation for our sins has been accepted. We have the freedom to live because of Christ today, knowing that this life has eternal value.

WHAT DO *YOU* THINK OF CHRIST?

- How often do you think of death? What emotions do you experience when thinking of it?

- Where do you seek an escape or solution to the problem of corruption?

- How does the realization of the pointlessness of trusting in Christ only in this earthly life change your perspective on life and your goals?

CHAPTER V
BORN TO ASCEND TO HEAVEN

... that enters into the inner place behind the curtain, where Jesus has gone as a forerunner on our behalf, having become a high priest forever after the order of Melchizedek. | Heb. 6:19–20

In previous chapters we discussed in sufficient detail several important reasons for divine incarnation. We have noted that the Son of God became man, first of all, to carry the sins of mankind and to die for them. Only a man with divine qualities was capable of this.

We also mentioned that the Son of God had to become incarnate to live a perfect, blameless life in our place so that afterwards this life could be credited to those who believe in Him.

Thirdly, we said that the Son of God became man so that, upon His resurrection as a man, He could overcome corruption and death — our bitterest enemies — and deliver us out of captivity to sin.

In this chapter we will look at one more blessing of divine incarnation that in its practical application is no less important that the ones discussed so far. Since His resurrection and return to heaven, Jesus Christ now stands in God's immediate presence as a man.

Let's look once again at the full panorama of what Paul called "the mystery of godliness."

> Great indeed, we confess, is the mystery of godliness:
>
> He was manifested in the flesh,
>   vindicated by the Spirit,
>   seen by angels,
> proclaimed among the nations,
>   believed on in the world,
>   **taken up in glory.** (1 Tim. 3:16)

Luke explains how Jesus Christ came to this earth.

> And the angel answered her, "The Holy Spirit will come upon you, and the power of the Most High will overshadow you." (Luke 1:35)

Christ was conceived by the work of the Holy Spirit in Mary's body. This God-Man was born and lived a life. He died. He was buried but rose from the dead. He did not remain on this earth in His glorified body — He went to heaven. But He did not simply go to heaven.

In the text above, Paul lists the ascension of Jesus Christ as the final glorious link in the great mystery of divine incarnation. It is the concluding phase of the grand-scale operation — code name "Redemption." Christ's ascension amazes us with its grandeur and glory no less than the incarnation or the resurrection.

The glorious mystery of ascension was that Jesus Christ went to heaven in a glorified physical body. His state and position in heaven are substantially different from what they were prior to the incarnation. The Son of God, the second Person of the Trinity, became the God-Man forever — he will never cease to be one. He exists in heaven in a physical body — and that is the mystery. As one of the unique aspects of divine incarnation celebrated on Christmas, it is a radical change in the essence of God's existence.

The Scripture gives multiple statements as proof of this glorious, mind-boggling mystery.

When Stephen was being stoned for preaching the Gospel, God showed Him special grace by opening the heavens. And when he looked up, he did not see a spirit, but the Son of Man standing at the right hand of God the Father.

> But he, full of the Holy Spirit, gazed into heaven and saw the glory of God, and Jesus standing at the right hand of God. And he said,
>
> **"Behold, I see the heavens opened, and the Son of Man standing at the right hand of God."** (Acts 7:55–56)

We're also told that when Jesus returns to earth, He will return as the God-Man.

> And when he had said these things, as they were looking on, he was lifted up, and a cloud took him out of their sight. And while they were gazing into heaven as he went, behold, two men stood by them in white robes, and said,
>
> "Men of Galilee, why do you stand looking into heaven? This Jesus, who was taken up from you into heaven, **will come in the same way** as you saw him go into heaven." (Acts. 1:9–11)

He will judge the world as the God-Man. He is the One Who has the right to say, "I have lived on earth. I know what it is like to be man. I have fulfilled My Father's will as man." His judgments are objective and just.

> And he has given him authority to execute judgment, **because he is the Son of Man.** (John 5:27)

Jesus Christ's physical ascension marked the final part of God's plan of redemption. Of course, earthly events continue, and one day the church will be united with her Lord. But the very act of redemption was complete at the precise moment of Jesus' ascension to heaven. In Jesus Christ, man was forever united with God.

Ascension is also the ultimate testimony to the faithfulness and unchangeable character of God's various blessings available to us through the incarnation. Having been united with Christ by being born again, we have become partakers of everything that belongs to Him. In this chapter we will take a closer look at some of the most significant blessings:

- Glorious body upon resurrection
- Inheritance in heaven
- Eternity spent in intimate fellowship with God

| TRANSFORMATION OF THE BODY |

Jesus Christ's ascension marked a new era in the history of mankind. We read about Enoch and Elijah, men who were taken up by God. But they were never placed on the level of the Trinity. When Jesus Christ became the God-Man, He did not take a place lower than the other two divine Persons. He returned as the Son of God. But He became the first Man to enter the immediate presence of the divine Trinity in an incorruptible body.

The ascension of Christ was testimony to the fact that the transformed body of the God-Man was so glorious that it was now capable of being in immediate unity with the divine Trinity. This is unique about the resurrection. Having risen from the grave, Jesus Christ defined a new kind of human existence in unity with God. This is a mystery.

> Great indeed, we confess, is the mystery of godliness:
>
> He was manifested in the flesh,
> > vindicated by the Spirit,
> > > seen by angels,
> >
> proclaimed among the nations,
> > believed on in the world,
> > > **taken up in glory.** (1 Tim. 3:16)

Ascension Day is a little known Christian holiday that gets lost among other big days of the year. Unfortunately, we don't appreciate the profound meaning behind this event. What the apostle calls "the great mystery of godliness" is not just another event. It is not just one of the miracles performed by Christ, like healing the sick or multiplying the bread. Jesus Christ performed an act of resounding significance in His ascension: He brought the human He had once created into a more perfect state than before the fall. He brought man into God's immediate presence! Christ glorified the human body by filling it with the glory of the Creator's nature. All of this is definitely beyond our imagination!

The nature-changing resurrection of the Son of God affects all born of the Holy Spirit, the church — Christ's bride and Christ's body. Everyone born of God will receive a glorified body, similar to Christ's, at the moment of his or her resurrection.

> So is it with the resurrection of the dead. What is sown is perishable; what is raised is imperishable. It is sown in dishonor; **it is raised in glory.** It is sown in weakness; it is raised in power. (1 Cor. 15:42–43)

This is what resurrection is all about, the essence of what the incarnate Son of God has achieved! He did not just come to live on this earth. He did not just come to teach people moral lessons. He came to radically transform their very being. This was the magnificent idea of God's plan! The Son of God crossed the line between the spiritual and the physical — He became man to elevate the humans living in the physical world to a higher dimension of existence.

Jesus mentioned many times during His life on earth that those who become His disciples will join Him in paradise. He spoke on this at length at His last supper with the disciples, repeatedly warning them that He would not be with them for a certain time, but that they would one day be together again:

> Little children, **yet a little while I am with you.** You will seek me, and just as I said to the Jews, so now I also say to you, 'Where I am going you cannot come.'
>
> A new commandment I give to you, that you love one another: just as I have loved you, you also are to love one another. By this all people will know that you are my disciples, if you have love for one another."
>
> Simon Peter said to him, "Lord, where are you going?"
>
> Jesus answered him, **"Where I am going you cannot follow me now, but you will follow afterward."** (John 13:33–36)

A little later, in John 14, Jesus addressed this topic again.

> Let not your hearts be troubled. Believe in God; believe also in me. In my Father's house are many rooms. If it were not so, would I have told you that I go to prepare a place for you? And if I go and prepare a place for you, I will come again and will take you to myself, that where I am you may be also. (John 14:1-3)

Some interpret these words to mean that Jesus Christ is now busy with an enormous construction project in heaven. People fantasize about angels creating heavenly megapolises in anticipation of the arrival of earthly inhabitants. My friends, God does not need much time to prepare a place for believers. The universe was formed by just one spoken word. This passage means something different.

Christ had to go through death and resurrection and enter heaven as a man to make way for His disciples — to prepare everything necessary so that we could later join Him! So, He explained that at that moment, His disciples could not follow Him. Only after the Holy Spirit came and the church was born would the place be ready for believers to join Him.

But the reason Christ has not come for His church yet is not that heavenly contractors are behind on the construction deadline. It's because He has a specific plan for those living on earth: He is waiting for the last of the Gentiles to be saved — to become part of His church (Rom. 11:25). But note — the place has already been prepared. And it was ready the moment Jesus entered heaven.

> "Let not your hearts be troubled. Believe in God; believe also in me. In my Father's house are many rooms. If it were not so, would I have told you that I go to prepare a place for you? And if I go and prepare a place for you, **I will come again and will take you to myself, that where I am you may be also.** (John 14:1–3)

John 17 holds another interesting detail of this revelation — our exact location once we are in heaven. In His high-priestly prayer spoken immediately after the last supper, Jesus addressed God with a petition concerning His disciples and all who would believe in Him.

> Father, **I desire that they also**, whom you have given me, **may be with me where I am.** (John 17:24)

He states here clearly that He wants those saved by Him to be present in heaven, and not in some obscure unknown place there, but in His very presence — for them to be right where He, their Lord, is.

> Father, I desire that they also, whom you have given me, may be with me where I am, **to see my glory that you have given me because you loved me** before the foundation of the world. (John 17:24).

The Greek word "see" (θεωρεω) in the original carries the meaning "to experience by paying close attention to something; to be filled by way of contemplation." In other words, Jesus' prayer to His Father was that those who would be saved through His sacrifice would *fully share* in His glory; that they would be filled with it, observe it, pay attention to it, closely contemplate the grandeur of the Son of God while in His immediate presence.

God answered this prayer. When Jesus Christ ascended to heaven as the God-Man, He opened the way for all those born of His Spirit. That is why, just like Him, we will receive immortal glorified bodies — bodies that are inextricably connected with the divine Trinity.

| HEAVENLY INHERITANCE |

The second blessing attested to by the physical ascension of Jesus Christ is the believers' inheritance that awaits them in heaven.

This is an awesome truth! Many people are used to talking about eschatological facts as something taken for granted: "saved, adopted, made heirs, will be raptured…" In reality, this is something much more complex and thrilling.

When apostle Peter comforted first-century believers undergoing persecution, hardships, and deprivation, he considered it his duty first to remind them that they have an inheritance in heaven.

> Blessed be the God and Father of our Lord Jesus Christ! According to his great mercy, he has caused us to be born again to a living hope through the

> resurrection of Jesus Christ from the dead, **to an inheritance that is imperishable, undefiled, and unfading, kept in heaven for you.** (1 Pet. 1:3–4)

Peter describes the heavenly inheritance as the destination for the children of God.

Our heavenly inheritance is a wonder unlike any other. An earthly inheritance, we know, is gathered by parents and passed to children at a certain time. If someone gives a part of their belongings to someone else, it is a generous gift, but not technically an inheritance. An inheritance is something that only belongs to a limited number of individuals endowed with corresponding rights.

Peter's message does not just mention gifts, crowns, awards, palaces, or streets of gold awaiting us in eternity — although those in themselves are a generous gift to former enemies of God! Instead, the Father promises us something that only belongs to His children, and it is amazing!

It is amazing because in the system of God's laws, everything must be taken into account, and justice must be served. In order for us to become heirs, it is not enough that God calls us such. We need to actually become His children.

Let's look at how God achieves this radical internal transformation.

BECOMING LIKE CHRIST

Salvation does not simply mean the change of a person's legal status according to the laws of heaven. It is a change of the person's nature. Basically, salvation only happens if one is born again.

When we talk about being born again, we are not talking about a special experience while hearing someone preach, or a person being really sorry about his sins, or someone praying very emotionally in a serious situation. Being born again implies a profound internal transformation. The person becomes different — new. Internally, this person acquires God's standards, God's purposes, God's desires. Now, he loves what God loves and wants what God wants.

In other words, those born of God's Spirit acquire a nature that is like Christ's. "Born again" is not a lofty Christian title — it is a second birth.

> For those whom he foreknew he also predestined to be conformed to the image of his Son, in order that he might be the firstborn among many brothers. (Rom. 8:29)

Jesus Christ came down to earth. It was an incredible act. He lived a full life yet without any sin. He died on the cross of Calvary in our place, rose again, and ascended to heaven. And through all that, there was a clear goal: not merely make us Christians, but to make us "conformed to the image of His Son, in order that He might be the firstborn among many brothers."

Many people are capable of radical change as a result of certain events. I have met unbelievers who have quit drinking and smoking and have become interested in things they'd never enjoyed before. White collar workers, criminals, atheists, Gentiles, poor or rich — all experience transformation. But the Scripture does not present personal transformation as a goal in and of itself. The Scripture talks about becoming Christ-like. It talks about someone who used to live in self-worship, but as a result of the work of the Holy Spirit experiences a second birth and becomes Christ-like in nature. This is the very purpose God has in giving people a second birth.

ADOPTED BY GOD

It is indeed possible to save man without adoption! People in the Garden of Eden were not children of God in the sense we are. They were God's creation. Unlike them, we are not just created beings — we are sinful creation. And in salvation, God did not just snatch us out of comdemnation. He also elevated us above the status of simple creation. He made us His children by way of the incarnation of Jesus Christ and baptizing us in Christ.

Adoption was a part of God's plan that was established even prior to the creation of the world:

> ...even as he chose us in him before the foundation of the world, that we should be holy and blameless before him. In love **he predestined us for adoption to himself as sons through Jesus Christ,** according to the purpose of his will. (Eph. 1:4–5)

Adoption is no less amazing than resurrection. In adopting us, God makes us, humans, His own sons and daughters!

> And we know that for those who love God all things work together for good, for those who are called according to his purpose. For those whom he foreknew he also predestined to be conformed to the image of his Son, **in order that he might be the firstborn among many brothers.** (Rom. 8:28-29)

Jesus Christ is the only begotten Son. But in this passage, we learn about God's astonishing plan: "in order that he might be the firstborn among many brothers." God makes people the body of Christ, His bride, one with the Lamb, baptizing them in Him.

Jesus is the firstfruits. He is the Redeemer, the One Who suffered for us — which will be fully obvious in eternity. And in our nature, we will be like Him — His brothers and sisters. Just like human nature became part of Christ's identity, Christ's nature defines the identity of a Christian. This is why it says in Romans,

> For we know that the whole creation has been groaning together in the pains of childbirth until now. And not only the creation, but **we ourselves, who have the firstfruits of the Spirit,** groan inwardly as we wait eagerly for adoption as sons, the redemption of our bodies. (Rom. 8:22-23)

Though we receive Christ's nature when we are born again, our identity remains closely associated with our flesh. This is the very reason of our internal struggle: We no longer want to live according to the law of the flesh; we have a relentless desire for God.

> For you did not receive the spirit of slavery to fall back into fear, but **you have received the Spirit of adoption as sons, by whom we cry, "Abba! Father!"**
>
> The Spirit himself bears witness with our spirit that we are children of God, and if children, then heirs — heirs of God and fellow heirs with Christ, provided we suffer with him in order that we may also be glorified with him. (Rom. 8:15-17)

"Abba! Father!" — with these words we run, walk, or even crawl to God because we are His seed (1 John 3:9). The firstfruits of the Spirit living in us incessantly draw us to the Source of all fullness.

We can compare this concept to a well-known natural law. In our region of the world, one of the leading industries in the economy is salmon farming. Anyone visiting salmon farms has a wonderful opportunity to observe the natural habits of this unusual fish.

Salmon are famous for covering thousands of miles to return to the place of their birth, and notably, they always do it by swimming against the current. This amazing determination is undeniable. Salmon will jump into the strongest whirlpool, risk their lives, die of wounds and wild beasts — they will even go on dry land attempting to cross the places where creeks have dried out — all to ultimately reach their birthplace and spawn there.

Salmon do this instinctively — because they are not perch or pike, but salmon. It is this nature, different from other fish, that draws them up the stream. It determines their behavior.

In this same manner, believers strive upwards toward God with all of their being, no matter the difficulties or even temptations that stand in their way. This spiritual instinct, this pull, defined by the new nature, is the driving force behind Christians' actions.

That is what distinguishes every true believer: Those born of God — no matter how many times they stumble, no matter the sin issues they struggle with, no matter the immaturity they try to overcome — will still be moving, whether running or crawling, towards Christ. The Spirit within them cries out, "Abba! Father!" They know there is nowhere else for them to go. God is their Father! And that is what adoption is all about. That is the transformation that Paul discusses.

Religious people get used to many terms. "Adoption" is one of them. When using the words "adoption," "born again," "heavenly inheritance," we often do not notice the mystery and true magnitude of these wonderful privileges. We almost take them for granted. But if you give this issue some profound thought, you will realize that adoption is an absolutely incredible phenomenon!

Before the creation of the world, before the first particle of the universe appeared, God prepared a plan. The central element of the process that followed was the creation of man in God's image and likeness. And we can see that man is, in fact, different from the rest of creation. He is created a person, and therefore is capable of fellowship with God. He can think, have self-awareness, and have awareness of God. He is capable of desires, evaluation, decision making, etc. Yet with all that, man is still a creation. Even before the fall, he was radically different from his perfect Creator.

God's design was that as a result of a long and complex chain of events, created humanity would become forever and inextricably united with Christ, and through Him, with God Himself.

God created man. He allowed for the fall to happen. But the story did not end there. God sent His Son to earth as the God-Man, inseparably unified with creation. And all this was to make humanity, through Christ, His true children. And Paul emphasizes that this was done exclusively by God's merciful initiative.

The implications of this phenomenon are impossible for the human mind to grasp. We have the hardest time comprehending how God could be an authentic man. But we have an even harder time understanding how humans could become true children of God.

In spite of all the inconceivability of adoption, God reveals to us certain aspects of it. For example, Romans explains that adoption happens as a result of being born of the Holy Spirit.

> For all who are led by the Spirit of God are sons of God. For you did not receive the spirit of slavery to fall back into fear, but **you have received the Spirit of adoption as sons, by whom we cry, "Abba! Father!"** The Spirit himself bears witness with our spirit that we are children of God. (Rom. 8:14–16)

In the Epistle to Galatians, Paul explains exactly how a person is born again.

> For **in Christ Jesus you are all sons of God, through faith.** For as many of you as were baptized into Christ have put on Christ. (Gal. 3:26–27)

The central piece of being born of the Spirit is faith, the practical entrusting of our lives to Jesus Christ: faith in the fact that we are all doomed sinners absolutely dependent on the kindness of God, and faith in the fact that He truly is the sense, the purpose, and the essence of everything in this world. As a result of this faith, we deny ourselves and lose ourselves in Christ. That is what makes us children of God.

> For as many of you as were baptized into Christ have put on Christ. (Gal. 3:27)

Being a Christian is not a lofty name. It is acquiring a new God-like nature.

COHEIRS WITH CHRIST

By acquiring Christ's nature and becoming true children of God, we also acquire the right to the inheritance God has prepared for His Son Jesus Christ. This is how Paul explains it:

> The Spirit himself bears witness with our spirit that we are children of God, **and if children, then heirs — heirs of God and fellow heirs with Christ,** provided we suffer with him in order that we may also be glorified with him. (Rom. 8:16–17)

Jesus Christ came to this earth so that, upon leaving, He could share His inheritance with a huge number of brothers among which He is the firstfruits. This is what divine incarnation is about. This is what is so unique. This is the mystery.

As a result of being born again, a Christian becomes a partaker of what belongs to God the Son, the second Person of the Trinity. But we need to keep in mind that these immeasurable riches are only available to us *in Christ*, in our unity with Him.

> Long ago, at many times and in many ways, God spoke to our fathers by the prophets, but in these last days he has spoken to us by **his Son, whom he appointed the heir of all things,** through whom also he created the world. (Heb. 1:1–2)

This passage tells us that everything in the universe belongs to the Son as His inheritance. And this means that Christ's fellow heirs will also inherit everything!

In a different passage, the Scripture talks about every blessing in heaven:

> Blessed be the God and Father of our Lord Jesus Christ, who has blessed us in Christ with **every spiritual blessing in the heavenly places**. (Eph. 1:3)

It is an amazing thing that God does not merely save us — feeble humans destined for eternal damnation. He does not merely make us Christlike. He does not merely make us His children. He also makes us full owners of all the best things He has created that he is passing on to His Son as an inheritance! And all this only because of the incarnation, life, death, resurrection, and ascension of Jesus Christ that we celebrate in this book.

In Galatians, Paul links all these elements of God's action plan together — from the incarnation through the inheritance:

> But when the fullness of time had come, God sent forth his Son, **born of woman** [came in the flesh], **born under the law** [lived a righteous life], **to redeem those who were under the law** [to die for them], so that **we might receive adoption as sons.**
>
> And because you are sons, God has sent the Spirit of his Son into our hearts, crying, "Abba! Father!" So you are no longer a slave, but a son, and if a son, then an **heir through God.** (Gal. 4:4–7)

| ETERNAL FELLOWSHIP WITH GOD |

The final blessing of the ascension Christ in His glorified body that we will examine in this book is that all true children of God receive through Him direct, never-ending fellowship with the Creator and the Master of the universe.

One of our most serious problems is a lack of connection with God. Man was created for fellowship with his Maker. We are totally dependent on Him. If we want to live and be happy, we all need constant, intimate contact with the Creator and the Source of our life.

Unfortunately, many people do not realize that. Instead of seeking fellowship with their Creator, they attempt to fill up the void in their hearts with something else: relationships, pleasure, acceptance among peers, etc. The Old Testament gives a perfect illustration of this.

> Be appalled, O heavens, at this; be shocked, be utterly desolate, declares the Lord, for my people have committed two evils: they have forsaken me, the fountain of living waters, and hewed out cisterns for themselves, broken cisterns that can hold no water. (Jer. 2:12–13)

Remember the failures that keep haunting you, the last situation where things did not go well, the plans that fell apart, when your hopes crashed? You need to realize that your true joy is in intimate fellowship with Christ.

The Scriptures abound with stories of people who experienced this closeness to God.

> O God, you are my God; earnestly I seek you; my soul thirsts for you; my flesh faints for you, as in a dry and weary land where there is no water. (Ps. 63:1)

David constantly sought God because he knew the true delight of fellowship with God.

> My soul will be satisfied as with fat and rich food, and my mouth will praise you with joyful lips, when I remember you upon my bed, and meditate on you in the watches of the night. (Ps. 63:5–6)

My friends, nothing is more precious than this here on earth! This is one of the most important goals of God's global plan. The Creator saved man to bring him into as intimate fellowship with Himself as possible. This was the very reason the new covenant was established.

> For this is the covenant that I will make with the house of Israel after those days, declares the Lord: I will put my law within them, and I will write it on their hearts. And **I will be their God, and they shall be my people.** (Jer. 31:33)

The purpose of the new covenant was to restore the harmony of a good, fatherly relationship between God and men — a relationship where people see Him as their Master, Lord, and Shepherd.

The history of God's relationship with mankind has four periods. (See image 2.)

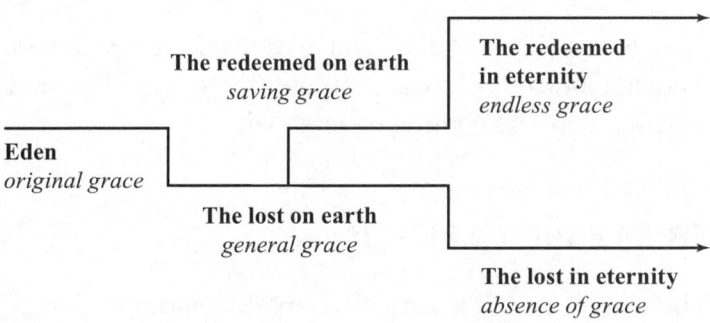

Levels of Fellowship with God
Image 2

THE EDEN PERIOD

The first humans, Adam and Eve, had a fairly free access to God. There was no sin yet that would separate them. They were able to be in the Lord's presence without any shame or fear. They could talk to Him and partner in various endeavors. That gave them a fullness of life, true joy, and happiness. The Eden period may be called the period of original grace.

But this fellowship was most likely not constant. In any case, at the time of being tempted, Adam and Eve were outside this fellowship, and once they sinned, the first humans began to avoid God.

> And they heard the sound of the Lord God walking in the garden in the cool of the day, **and the man and his wife hid themselves from the presence of the Lord God** among the trees of the garden. (Gen. 3:8)

This is proof that Adam and Eve, even being sinless, were not joined to God and His nature the way it became possible with the coming of Jesus Christ.

FROM FALL TO DEATH

The fall radically changed people's relationship with God. First, as we have already noted, people put themselves in a position of being God's opponents. Fellowship with God was no longer desirable. But the most dreadful thing is that God wouldn't even allow sinful men into His circle.

> Then the Lord God said, "Behold, the man has become like one of us in knowing good and evil. Now, lest he reach out his hand and take also of the

> tree of life and eat, and live forever — " therefore the Lord God sent him out from the garden of Eden to work the ground from which he was taken. (Gen. 3:22–23)

From then on, man has been doomed to an eternal search for happiness, but he cannot and does not want to turn to its source — God.

> And **you were dead** in the trespasses and sins in which you once walked, following the course of this world, following the prince of the power of the air, the spirit that is now at work **in the sons of disobedience** — among whom we all once lived **in the passions of our flesh, carrying out the desires of the body and the mind,** and were by nature children of wrath, like the rest of mankind. (Eph. 2:1–3)

This is a state of spiritual death, a disconnectedness from the Source of life, a state of being enslaved by own lusts. Everyone this side of paradise experiences this alienation from the life of God.

> Now this I say and testify in the Lord, that you must no longer walk as the Gentiles do, in the futility of their minds. They are darkened in their understanding, alienated from the life of God because of the ignorance that is in them, due to their hardness of heart. (Eph. 4:17–18)

But this level of relationship with God is not the most tragic possible. It is not the end. It is not a final moment when God forever isolates Himself from people. Today, in spite of human sinfulness, God is still pouring out His grace on all who live on this earth. The following are but a few examples of this grace.

God maintains life on earth

> For he makes his sun rise on the evil and on the good, and sends rain on the just and on the unjust. (Matt. 5:45)

The fact that the earth still spins, the sun shines, our hearts keep beating, our bodies function, and our minds think — all of this is evidence of God's grace.

This world is His, and it operates according to His laws. God is in no way obliged to provide any kind of good things for us. And our rebellion against our Creator, as evidenced by the fall, demands punishment from God, not provision and good things. But, because of His love, God continues to maintain life on earth, providing us with all of the essentials.

God gives us the opportunity to turn back

> And he made from one man every nation of mankind to live on all the face of the earth, having determined allotted periods and the boundaries of their dwelling place, that they should seek God, and perhaps feel their way toward him and find him. (Acts 17:26–27)

People simply do not want to turn to God. They avoid Him, yet He continues telling them of Himself and offering them opportunities to seek Him. In one of his sermons, Paul said,

> We...bring you good news, that you should turn from these vain things to a living God, who made the heaven and the earth and the sea and all that is in them. In past generations he allowed all the nations to walk in their own ways. **Yet he did not leave himself without witness, for he did good** by giving you rains from heaven and fruitful seasons, satisfying your hearts with food and gladness. (Acts 14:15-17)

God continues calling out to people, communicating with mankind. The natural world that surrounds us is a vivid testimony to its Creator's existence. Anyone in their right mind can see that the One Who created the universe is extremely intelligent, extremely powerful, and extremely good.

So, the way to God is wide open! The only reason people do not want to go God's way is their unwillingness to acknowledge God's authority and to bow down before Him.

God receives repentant sinners

God is still in the business of salvation! And this is what is most precious. The Holy Spirit still works in human hearts; the door of salvation is still open.

> For there is no distinction between Jew and Greek; for the same Lord is Lord of all, bestowing his riches on all who call on him. For "everyone who calls on the name of the Lord will be saved." (Rom. 10:12–13)

But note that all three kinds of grace just discussed will be taken from mankind as soon as the final line is drawn.

THE EARTHLY LIFE OF THE REDEEMED

The third level of relationship with God exists simultaneously with the second but is radically different. It is the relationship of God with those who have turned to Him through Jesus Christ.

Believers continue living on earth but already enjoy access to fellowship with God. They know God as their Father; they are drawn to Him. They are confident that the Father accepts them, that He is their safe place. He understands them, He will take care of them, He is able to forgive them, and He will support them.

Redeemed people treasure their relationship with God. They value His word. They want to hear Him and spend time in prayer. And yes, these believers still walk this earth and continue experiencing pain, suffering, and pressure from their sinful flesh. Sometimes they stumble and lose the state of connectedness to God because, in spite of having God's life in them, their fellowship with God is still limited by a sinful physical body. But they understand a sweet fellowship with the Father! They have "tasted that the Lord is good."

These are people who have been transformed from God's enemies to His friends thanks to the sacrifice of the Son that paid their debt.

> And you, **who once were alienated and hostile in mind,** doing evil deeds, he has now reconciled in his body of flesh by his death, in order to present you holy and blameless and above reproach before him. (Col. 1:21–22)

They have been liberated by God and have become full citizens of the Kingdom of Heaven.

> … giving thanks to the Father, who has qualified you to share in the inheritance of the saints in light. He has delivered us from the domain of darkness and transferred us to the kingdom of his beloved Son. (Col. 1:12–13)

They are God's now — members of His household.

> So then you are no longer strangers and aliens, but you are fellow citizens with the saints and members of the household of God. (Eph. 2:19)

God's children have firsthand experience of fellowship with God. And it does not matter whether they have a *profound understanding of the Scriptures, whether they can define doctrines, or whether they only know* John 3:16 and have realized that Christ is their Savior. The key fact is that they have experienced a saving relationship with God. Yes, this knowledge is limited by earthly life, but it is there, as Paul describes it:

> For now we see in a mirror dimly, but then face to face. Now I know in part; then I shall know fully, even as I have been fully known. (1 Cor. 13:12)

The transformation of our body and the rapture to heaven at Christ's second coming will complete our liberation from all obstacles standing in the way of our fellowship with God today.

> Beloved, we are God's children now, and what we will be has not yet appeared; but we know that when he appears, we shall be like him, because we shall see him as he is. (1 John 3:2)

There is nothing more satisfying, more rewarding for Christians than intimate fellowship with their Lord.

But whatever gain I had, I counted as loss for the sake of Christ. Indeed, I count everything as loss because of the surpassing worth of knowing Christ Jesus my Lord. For his sake I have suffered the loss of all things and count them as rubbish, in order that I may gain Christ. (Phil. 3:7–8)

"To gain Christ" in this passage is not the same as "to be saved." By the time Paul wrote these lines, he had already been saved. But Paul had a burning desire to have an ever-deepening relationship with Christ. He wanted to be filled with Him more and more, be brought into the reality of Christ's presence, have His desires, submit to His will. This is why he says, "Everything I left behind is rubbish. I have tasted something that is immeasurably better!"

My friends, I want to urge you to hold dear your fellowship with God, — hold it in the highest esteem possible! Do not allow any other area of your life to become more important than your fellowship with Him. No matter how important your work or obligations may be, no matter how noble your intentions, no matter how stressful the circumstances... Do not allow relationships, work, health issues or anything else to interrupt the lifeblood of your fellowship with God! It represents the saving grace operating in the lives of believers.

ETERNITY

Eternity is the part of human existence that begins after death and stretches out into infinity. In eternity, the character of people's relationship with God will differ drastically from all that we know now. It will also be divided into two categories: eternity in hell and eternity in paradise. These are the two states where grace will reach its ultimate limits.

The lost: An eternity without fellowship with God

First, let us look at those who will spend eternity persisting in their rebellion against God.

While living on earth, people still have access to God's universal grace although they may resist it.

> For the wrath of God is revealed from heaven against all ungodliness and unrighteousness of men, who by their unrighteousness suppress the truth.
>
> For what can be known about God is plain to them, because God has shown it to them.
>
> For his invisible attributes, namely, his eternal power and divine nature, have been clearly perceived, ever since the creation of the world, in the things that have been made. So they are without excuse. (Rom. 1:18-20)

They have no excuse and no way out of it: God's presence in this world and the attributes of His character are shouting at them in creation. These people use various ideas in an attempt to disprove this truth, suppress it, silence it. But if they die, or if the Lord's coming catches them off guard, the opportunity to be saved will be lost to them forever.

This is the drastic difference between eternity and the previous periods. In eternity, the general, universal grace will end. It will be reduced to nothing. There will be no more joy, peace, or hope.

People are used to enjoying the benefits of earthly life, and they don't even consider the fact that all of them flow from God's grace. But once they cross the great divide, the unsaved are suddenly faced with the reality of God — now their Enemy and Judge. And that is the horrible tragedy of hell — the disappearance of God's favor and the absolute lack of any hope of reconciliation with the Source of life. The horror of eternal dying without the possibility of death — this is how the book of Revelation describes these final events in the history of the world:

> And the devil who had deceived them was thrown into the lake of fire and sulfur where the beast and the false prophet were, and **they will be tormented day and night forever and ever.**
>
> Then I saw a great white throne and him who was seated on it. From his presence earth and sky fled away, and no place was found for them.
>
> And I saw the dead, great and small, standing before the throne, and books were opened. Then another book was opened, which is the book of life. And the dead were judged by what was written in the books, according to what they had done.
>
> And the sea gave up the dead who were in it, Death and Hades gave up the dead who were in them, and they were judged, each one of them, according to what they had done. Then Death and Hades were thrown into the lake of fire. This is the second death, the lake of fire.
>
> **And if anyone's name was not found written in the book of life, he was thrown into the lake of fire.** (Rev. 20:10–15)

Notice how it says here, "the second death," meaning the final separation of man from God. The essence of the final punishment for those who did not humble themselves before God, those who did not accept His saving grace while on earth, is their absolute loss of this grace forever.

Man was created for fellowship with God. The less of this fellowship he has, the more intolerable his life. And when fellowship with God is cut off entirely, an irrevocable catastrophe follows. As a fish cast out on the shore, man will be deprived of the Source of life — for eternity.

The redeemed: Eternity in intimate fellowship with God

The status of the redeemed in eternity will be drastically different from that of the unsaved. For the unbeliever, crossing over into eternity cuts off all hope for God's grace, but for the saved, death opens wide the doors to paradise. For believers, eternity means absolute, unlimited, never-ending, ultra-close fellowship with their Lord, Creator, and Savior. This is for God's children — His heirs, carriers of His nature, those whose spirit cries out "Abba! Father!" All these good things are a direct result of the glorious incarnation of Jesus Christ!

> For the Lord himself will descend from heaven with a cry of command, with the voice of an archangel, and with the sound of the trumpet of God. And the dead **in Christ** will rise first. Then we who are alive, who are left, will be caught up together with them in the clouds to meet the Lord in the air, **and so we will always be with the Lord.** (1 Thess. 4:16–17)

The dead and the living who are "in Christ" will join Him. Thanks to the incarnation of the Son of God, thanks to His life, death, resurrection, and ascension into the Father's presence, we will forever be with the Lord.

The last phrase in this passage carries the heaviest meaning. Look at what it means to "be with the Lord." The book of Revelation gives an amazing description of the future life in heaven…

> And I heard a loud voice from the throne saying, "Behold, the dwelling place of God is with man. He will dwell with them, and they will be his people, and God himself will be with them as their God.
>
> He will wipe away every tear from their eyes, and death shall be no more, neither shall there be mourning, nor crying, nor pain anymore, for the former things have passed away." (Rev. 21:3–4)

The first thing John heard the voice say was, "Behold, the dwelling place of God is with man" — that is, the place where God lives is with men. But it is a highly unusual statement.

We know that when the Lord descended on Mount Sinai, the Israelites trembled and were afraid to approach the mountain. People begged Moses, "You go up to the mountain because we are scared." And when God's presence filled the central part of the Temple, called the Holy of Holies, the Law gave a stern warning that no one was to enter behind the curtain. Only once a year, after a complex ceremony, the high priest could stand in that space before God and remain alive.

But now, we read in this passage that there will be a place where God is revealed and available to people! "God's dwelling place with men" is the greatest good available to the inhabitants of the universe. And this is why Christ came in the flesh!

To convey more clearly the beauty of this fellowship, the voice says, "and God will wipe away every tear." Heavenly fellowship with the Lord will completely obliterate the last trace of any sadness and worry that the children of God are subjected to at present.

The saved will be His people, and He will be their God, and in this is the amazing blessing of heaven! The blessing that became accessible thanks to the fact that Jesus assumed human flesh, lived a holy life in our place, died as punishment for our sins, rose to overcome corruption and death, and ascended to heaven where He now awaits us in the new Jerusalem. He is waiting for us to share with Him His and our inheritance. He waits for us to come enjoy this amazing, never-ending happiness — the happiness of fellowship with the perfect and incredible God! Our God.

WHAT DO *YOU* THINK OF CHRIST?

- How does the realization that one day He will transform your body "to conform to His glorious body" help you to overcome daily difficulties, suffering, and sickness?

- Why is fellowship with God the greatest treasure in the world?

- Evaluate your own efforts to count everything as loss "because of the surpassing worth of knowing Christ."

CHAPTER VI
BORN TO SAVE

"For God so loved the world,
that he gave his only Son, that
whoever believes in him should
not perish but have eternal life." | John 3:16

For many companies, Christmas has become a stepping-stone on their way to commercial success. Their revenue in the holiday season alone often equals the total annual volume of sales. Corporations evaluate Christmas by the amount of money people spend at the stores. So, I was surprised when I read recently statistics that 68% of the population of the United States refers to Christmas specifically as the birth of Jesus the Savior. (Of course, it is a mystery how the overwhelming majority of those polled in the same survey also does not believe that Jesus existed as a historical figure.)

But still, if 68% of the population of the country acknowledge that Christmas is the birth of the Savior,

I cannot help but ask, why are the saved so few? And those who are not saved, why do they celebrate it?

Why does salvation remain something distant, academic, churchy? Why isn't it something real, relevant, emotional, life-changing? If this holiday affects so many people, then why does Jesus Christ not become part of the decision-making process? Why does Jesus Christ have no effect on the morality of these people? Why does Christ not rule in their emotions and feelings? Why does He not determine the realities of a society that celebrates Him? Something does not add up…

It is amazing: People wish each other peace, kindness, love — and ignore the Source of these things! Why do people settle for the external effect of this holiday, but not let it go deeper, into their hearts?

Why is it that even many Christians do not really know the power of God incarnate? Why, when giving each other Christmas greetings and singing songs about it, do they keep on living as if Christ never came? Why is it that when they talk about Christmas, they remember, at best, the star and the Infant, the angels and the shepherds, the magi and their gifts? They recite these events as if they were a beautiful fairy tale that, even if based on some real events, happened so long ago that it no longer determines the purpose and meaning of their daily lives.

This chapter, like a powerful light, is meant to illuminate for every one of us the primary striking truth concealed in the Christmas events — the truth that is expressed in one well-known Bible verse. Those who have at least a superficial knowledge of the Bible could probably recite this without thinking. Unfortunately, few realize the depth of its meaning.

> For God so loved the world, that he gave his only Son, that whoever believes in him should not perish but have eternal life. (John 3:16)

These words were spoken by Jesus Himself, and I want to suggest that you look at this amazing verse from Christ's perspective. What was the context for these words? What did our Lord want to emphasize when He made this monumental statement? It is my prayer that as you approach the end of this chapter, you become partakers of the colossal treasure concealed in the fact of the Messiah's coming to this earth.

| FAITH THAT DOES NOT SAVE |

These famous words of Christ were spoken in a conversation with a Jewish teacher and a member of Sanhedrin, Nicodemus.

> Now there was a man of the Pharisees named Nicodemus, a ruler of the Jews. This man came to Jesus by night. (John 3:1,2)

What is curious is that this man, a Pharisee, was willing to set aside his religious knowledge and come to Jesus to learn from Him. He was willing to ignore public opinion and that of his colleagues. It is obvious that he did not want to be associated with Christ, which is why he came in secret, by night. But he was interested enough to even come in the first place!

> This man came to Jesus by night and said to him,
>
> "Rabbi, we know that you are a teacher come from God, for no one can do these signs that you do unless God is with him." (John 3:2)

Nicodemus acknowledged (unlike many others) that Jesus had come from God. He was humble enough, in spite of his high standing, to admit Christ's supremacy over him.

It is likely he was a good man, and the sincere spiritual pursuit was part of his experience. He was looking to solve the issue of man's relationship with God. It was not merely a philosophical question. Nicodemus was a devout Jew — a Pharisee. This implies that he dedicated extended periods of time to profound study of the Law. He was a man who, while studying it, was eager to live by its precepts and taught others to do the same.

And this was the reason he came to see Christ. He came to find the missing piece in the puzzle of his worldview. But Jesus' conversation with this extraordinary man revealed that Nicodemus had not found salvation, at least not by that moment. He still remained disconnected from the Source of grace.

This was unexpected! Anyone else could remain unsaved, but not Nicodemus! This diligent man who spent so much time learning God's will! Others, yes. Criminals, hypocrites... They were lacking the very longing for God. But Nicodemus was a sincere man who came straight to the Son of God Himself, eager to hear His advice!

In this, Nicodemus is very much like modern-day religious people, gathering over Christmas in churches and sincerely admiring the masterpieces created by Christian composers. They are happy to be in the company of devout people. They feel good as they sing, "Joy to the world! The Lord is come!" But, like Nicodemus, they have never experienced the true effect of Jesus Christ. They have not realized that this Infant was born to *save them*.

The rabbi's problem was not insufficient knowledge or lack of works. Nicodemus' problem was a misguided approach to God.

Without introduction, Christ drew Nicodemus's attention to the central element of man's relationship with God: being born from above. Without it, the rest would be empty rhetoric.

> Jesus answered, "Truly, truly, I say to you, unless one is born of water and the Spirit, he cannot enter the kingdom of God. That which is born of the flesh is flesh, and that which is born of the Spirit is spirit." (John 3:5–6)

If you notice, Christ did not even mention the Law, or the accuracy of interpretation of prophetic texts, or the number of commandments. He understood that in this situation, none of that was relevant. He presented him with a dilemma: If you're not born again, you cannot see the Kingdom of God. No one can.

> Nicodemus said to him, "How can these things be?"
>
> Jesus answered him, "Are you the teacher of Israel and yet you do not understand these things?
>
> Truly, truly, I say to you, we speak of what we know, and bear witness to what we have seen, but you do not receive our testimony. If I have told you earthly things and you do not believe, how can you believe if I tell you heavenly things? (John 3:9–12)

The idea of being born from above was absolutely foreign to Nicodemus. It did not fit his model of the world, the one built on the premise that the person trying to please God had more chances to be saved than one who did not care about the Law. Nicodemus had come to make sure his efforts would pay off. And here, Jesus asked only one, bizarre yet unambiguous question: "Are you born from above?"

The truth of being born again was entirely new for Nicodemus, in spite of him being a teacher of Jewish Law. To help Nicodemus and those like him understand, Jesus gave a definition of what it means to be born from above, as well as the purpose of His coming to earth.

> For God so loved the world, that he gave his only Son, **that whoever believes in him should not perish but have eternal life.** (John 3:16)

In recent years, people have worn pins at this time of year that say, "It's okay to wish me a Merry Christmas.[11]" They fight for Christmas to continue being accepted in society. Unfortunately, it is likely that Christmas for these people is just a holiday, devoid of deeper meaning, of its true significance. The reason for the Messiah's coming to earth has never become clear for them and never become a life-defining factor. It's like it exists in a parallel world — just like Nicodemus and the Son of God.

The Jewish teacher possessed vast knowledge of the Law. But it did not save him. Nicodemus' problem was his wrong approach to the Son of God. Notice Jesus' rebuke:

> Truly, truly, I say to you, we speak of what we know, and bear witness to what we have seen, but **you do not receive our testimony.** (John 3:11).

It was not the first time that Nicodemus had heard Jesus speak. He knew Christ called Himself the Son of God. He knew that He insisted on the complete depravity of man and his need of a Savior. The problem was not that he did not know all these things. The problem was that,

---

[11] "It's okay to wish me a Merry Christmas!" pins appeared in the USA in recent years when political correctness began bordering on the absurd and instead of "Merry Christmas," many began saying, "Happy Holidays."

while listening to God incarnate, he did not believe His words! He did not take them seriously, not enough to allow them to change his life!

That night, in His response to Nicodemus, Jesus stated five truths that define the essence of salvation. Five crucial elements of the Gospel of Christmas. Five crucial elements of Christianity — your Christianity, too, if you have been born again.

| ACKNOWLEDGING THE NEED |

The Gospel starts with nothing less than a need of salvation. God came to earth precisely because people are perishing.

One of the main problems Nicodemus faced, just like you and I face today, was that he did not realize how hopeless his situation was. We usually think that our lives are basically okay, except for some minor issues: health problems, marital problems, financial instability. And though often such problems pile up, people continue thinking that it is all about the quality of life, about various external factors, but not about the internal problems of their own souls.

We often quote the line, "Jesus came to save the lost.[12]" And we are all for Christ saving the lost! But I think we have a difficult time tying the meaning of these words with our own identity.

---

[12] Matt. 18:11

Jesus states, "I came to save men *from perishing!*"

> For God so loved the world, that he gave his only Son, that whoever **believes in him** should not perish but have eternal life. (John 3:16)

This was Nicodemus' problem. He came to Christ as a confident, self-sufficient religious man. He came to discuss spirituality, religious needs of his time, right and superior things. He did not come to Christ as a lost sinner. Far from it. Who are you calling "lost"? Him? A teacher in Israel?!

And there you have it — the biggest problem of modern Christianity, the main reason why millions sing, "We wish you a Merry Christmas!" yet remain unsaved.

Just like Nicodemus, people do not mind adding Jesus with His moral code to what they already have. But to acknowledge that they are lost? Are you out of your mind? It's humiliating. It's rude!

Who are you calling lost? Nicodemus and those like him?! They are the Sanhedrin Members of the Year (if there were such a thing)! They are our best people! They are our spiritual heroes. Are they lost?! Yet Jesus's words are clear, "God so loved the world and gave His only Son" for one purpose, and one only: "so that whoever *believes ... should not perish*."

The Greek verb "ἀπόλλυμι", which means "to destroy or annihilate" is used in this sentence in medio-passive voice which indicates that the sinful man is in the process of self-destruction. In other words, he is digging his own grave. His demise is not due to external factors — it comes from inside.

In order to help Nicodemus to have a better grasp on this concept, Jesus reminds him of the story of God saving Israelites from death after they had been bitten by venomous serpents sent as punishment for their sin.

> And as Moses lifted up the serpent in the wilderness, so must the Son of Man be lifted up. (John 3:14)

A man bitten by a serpent was on his way to death. He was still walking, seeing, talking, but he was already dying. This is the state all men are in today. They think they are alive, but they are actually dying a slow death.

The only means of salvation that God gave for the serpent-bitten was the chance to look at the bronze serpent set on a pole and remain alive. Salvation was impossible without understanding the gravity of one's situation, which was imminent death. And salvation without realizing the gravity of one's problem is impossible today as well. Christ said,

> "Those who are well have no need of a physician, but those who are sick. I came not to call the righteous, but sinners." (Mark 2:17)

So, in answer to the question posed earlier — why people who are so close to Jesus Christ remain unsaved — we have discovered the first reason: They do not admit they are lost. They want to give gifts, talk about the Baby Jesus, decorate Christmas trees, participate in programs, discuss family values, love, and magic…. But they cannot stand it if someone so much as hints that they are lost, helpless, and in need of a Savior. Yet it is only for the sake of these that Christ came.

> For the Son of Man came to save the lost. (Matt. 18:11)

People like to make themselves look a little nobler than they are and change their habits a little, but they don't want to admit their utter spiritual and moral ruin. That is why I want to ask you, do you admit you are a hopeless sinner? Do you realize that the Savior came to snatch you out of hell? To save you from a real, eternal death, not an imaginary one? If you do not admit the fact that you are lost, your Christmas joy will never rise above enjoyment of beautiful music.

| THE SAVIOR'S MOTIVATION |

Nicodemus came to Christ, but he had his own "source of salvation": his religious works and righteousness. Jesus rejected this approach outright, stating in an unambiguous way that the only reason for salvation is God's love:

> **For God so loved the world,** that he gave his only Son, that whoever believes in him should not perish but have eternal life. (John 3:16)

Everything indicates that Nicodemus was very diligent in keeping the commandments. He was probably in the top 1% of the most pious people in Israel — the most sincere, the most zealous. He alone came to Christ among all the teachers, Pharisees, scribes, Jewish rulers! He did not come to argue, but to learn how to better please God! And Christ pulled the carpet out from under him!

But Christ's goodness is in this very thing. Our salvation does not come from our own achievements. Salvation is not initiated by the religious or "piously inclined" people. Salvation proceeds from one place only: God's loving heart. Jesus explained to Nicodemus, "It is not that you are such a good person. Everyone, including you, is condemned. It is God Who loves the world so much. That is what matters!"

If it were not for the great, incomprehensible love of God, man would have been eternally lost back at the point of the fall. Only because of His amazing love did God offer a plan of redemption. Only thanks to God's great love is the world still in existence. Thanks to this same love, God's only Son came to earth in human flesh. Only because of the Creator's great love was the Calvary sacrifice offered to satisfy God's demand for justice. There were no other reasons.

God had no obligations whatsoever to even move a finger to save mankind. This sincere, warm love had no other motivation than God's will. God loved us *in spite* of all our horrible sin. It was His decision to become the Savior of men. Not our piousness, nor our noble morality, nor our charitable actions, nor our strict rules, nor the level of our involvement in the church — nothing but His love is the source of our salvation.

We were forewarned of the dangers of sin. God said, "If you taste of the fruit of the tree, you will surely die." It was not a curse or a sentence; it was a mere statement of the facts. Just like AIDS guarantees death, sin dooms man to eternal damnation.

But God, in His great love, began a most astonishing operation of redemption. This operation cost Him very dearly. It cost Him incarnation, a difficult life in the realities of the fallen world, and a death on a cross. He who looks for reasons for God's favor in any other factors loses the only hope of salvation.

| THE MEANS OF SALVATION |

Further in John 3, Christ indicates the means of salvation: "God… gave His Son."

> For God so loved the world, **that he gave his only Son**, that whoever believes in him should not perish but have eternal life. (John 3:16)

I want to draw our attention to the word "gave." What does it mean, "He gave"?

Naturally, none of us would give our son to death. I cannot imagine a father who could give his son even for heroes who've done great things, let alone for criminals!

But for God to give His Son meant much more than what we can really conceive.

God the Father and God the Son are one. They are inseparably united in the divine Trinity. When God gave His Son, He continued to experience all the pain, all the pressure, all the feelings, all the tension — everything the Son experienced on earth. It was not a one-time gift. It was a living, continual process where the Father experienced all the trials the Son was going through.

Did you ever see your children suffer — from sickness, or offence, or humiliation? I am sure you were willing to burn with the fever or twist in pain (physical or emotional) just to spare your child this evil.

The Father experienced the Son's pain with all of His soul, and yet, quite consciously, did nothing to stop His suffering because it was the price to be paid for redemption — yours and mine.

| THE METHOD OF SALVATION |

The fourth element of our salvation is the method of achieving it. After describing the heavenly angle, Christ went on to the earthly. He explained how exactly the salvation accomplished by the Son of God becomes available to men — what specifically is needed for a person to be saved.

> For God so loved the world, **that he gave his only Son**, that whoever believes in him should not perish but have eternal life. (John 3:16)

Jesus emphasized that God loved the whole world, meaning that the whole world experiences the effects of the universal grace of God, but it does not necessarily follow that the entire world will be saved. Only those will be saved who "believe in Him." This is why it is so crucial to know if you believe or not. If you do not believe, you are lost. If you believe, you are saved!

And here, it is extremely important to have the right understanding of what it means to believe. Some think that you only need to acknowledge the fact that Christ lived on this earth. Others go further, agreeing that believers need to understand He was also the Savior of the world. Another group says that those who believe must have been baptized and belong to a Christian church. Still others insist that believers must be religiously active, participate in church life, and enjoy religious discussions. And all of the above is good and necessary, but faith is more than this. All these people, like Nicodemus, still lack something.

> Nicodemus said to him, "How can these things be?"
>
> Jesus answered him, "Are you the teacher of Israel and yet you do not understand these things? Truly, truly, I say to you, we speak of what we know, and bear witness to what we have seen, but you do not receive our testimony.
>
> If I have told you earthly things and you do not believe, how can you believe if I tell you heavenly things?" (John 3:9–12)

In this passage, "we" refers to God the Father, God the Son, and God the Holy Spirit. Jesus spoke on behalf of the divine Trinity. You would think Nicodemus would jump for joy due to the fact that God Himself was explaining to him the way of salvation! He came from the place Nicodemus was eager to get to, and He spoke of that which He only knew. But Jesus stated another fact: "You do not receive our testimony." And so, this intelligent man with high moral standards remained unsaved while speaking to the Savior Himself!

Nicodemus knew much of the Law. But when Jesus began testifying to what God is like and how He is planning to save mankind, Nicodemus could not make sense of it. When faced with something beyond his understanding, he refused to receive it. In Nicodemus' eyes, Jesus Christ possessed the knowledge, but not the divine authority. Nicodemus considered himself the measure of all things. The words of Christ had no more weight for him than the opinion of any other rabbi.

If you were to walk down the street today and meet Nicodemus, what would you say of him? Does he believe or not? He doesn't deny God — that is for sure. He honors God's Law, he teaches it, he participates in the activities organized by the Sanhedrin and the Temple. He is not just a believer — he is a super-believer! But Nicodemus has a problem that Christ says defines what he is: He does not receive the testimony of Jesus Christ.

Dear friends, your faith is only strong to the degree you seriously accept God's testimony. Whether you are a believer or not is determined by one thing only: Do you acknowledge God's authority, do you trust His word, and do you respond to it the way God expects you to?

Faith is not mere agreement with the fact that God exists. Faith is the acceptance of the authority of God's Word, trusting it in practical matters. Many religious people are willing to admit God exists, but they do not want to take His word seriously. They are not willing to acknowledge the power and authority of the Creator of the world behind these words.

Nicodemus believed, but there was something wrong with his faith. It included much activity and religious appearance. But with all that, he still believed on his own terms.

Even today, there are many who say, "I have my own beliefs." Did you ever think how foolish these words actually are? Imagine driving on the road according to your own rules, and you are stopped by a police officer. He will evaluate you by the objective rules of the law, not yours! In a similar way, people say they "believe" but get very offended if you tell them they are lost sinners in violation of God's Law and in need of a Savior!

The problem is that as long as we do not believe the way God intended, we will remain unsaved. No matter how much we celebrate Christmas, no matter how much we talk about being sincere or spiritual, no matter what great deeds we accomplish for humanity's sake — without true faith, we can never achieve salvation.

Christ gives a warning — "that whoever believes in him should not perish but have eternal life." Do you believe in Him? Have you truly bowed down before the authority of the word of the Son of God recorded in the Bible? Do you acknowledge its objective truthfulness? Do you realize that you are a ruined sinner, deserving of punishment? Does this realization break your heart? Does it motivate you to rush to the Son of God to obtain undeserved mercy and forgiveness? Are you willing to implore Christ to save you because you are utterly incapable of saving yourself? Do you believe "in Him," in Christ, the Lamb of God crucified for your sins? Do you believe in Him as the Lord Whose word is to be obeyed — the Lord to Whom you are willing to dedicate your entire life?

| THE PURPOSE OF SALVATION |

The last thing Jesus draws Nicodemus' attention to while witnessing to him about salvation was its result:

> "For God so loved the world, that he gave his only Son, that whoever believes in him should not perish **but have eternal life.** (John 3:16)

Every one of us, without a shadow of doubt, needs salvation from damnation. But God does so much more through His Son. Christ does not promise "that whoever believes in him should not perish but keep on living a more or less tolerable life." Jesus gives life. Life that never ends! This is the happiness Christmas brings!

Christian salvation is more than just salvation from shame and hell. Jesus saves you and me to make us new people — loving God, finding pleasure in Him, holding dear His truth, eager to obey Him. It is only possible under one condition — that we be born again. Only then do we acquire Jesus Christ's nature.

Eternal life is a life filled with profound peace, life filled with heavenly joy, life in God's presence that will never be taken away. It is real, happy, eternal life! Do you have this life?

***

Every contact with God's greatness and His inconceivability inevitably fills us with awe. If you truly seek God, if you do not settle for mere singing of Christmas carols but think of Whom you sing, and if you do not simply listen to sermons but try to comprehend the depth of the word being preached, then you are faced with the fact that you are a small, feeble human — a person very limited in ability to comprehend all of this. Yet the great Creator addresses you directly. He speaks to you through His Son Who became Man.

It inspires admiration because God is so big, so majestic, and so much more intelligent than we are. This brings us joy and gives us confidence and satisfaction. Why? Because thanks to the greatest sacrifice of the incarnate Son, we know that this incredible God is our good Shepherd, our Father, and we can safely trust Him.

Some people say that if we emphasize the greatness of God, we humiliate man. Quite the contrary! Only when we believe in the great God can man truly rest confidently in Him. He is, in fact, able to put his trust in the One Who is higher, stronger, kinder, and more just than anyone else. The divine incarnation has demonstrated that it is truly so.

Christmas is one of the most striking presentations of the inconceivability of God. This commonplace holiday puts us face to face with the astonishing greatness of the Creator. It is the celebration of the time when God became Man, when this limitless Spirit that exceeds human intellectual comprehension (for God is a Spirit) assumed human flesh. And He did not become a human just to do so, but in order to redeem you and me. This is why Christmas is not just an explosion of emotions. It is our response to God's inconceivability — our response of worship.

Is this your response?

We began our journey at the Temple entrance where disgruntled Pharisees made great effort to undermine Christ's reputation. In response to their hate-filled questions, Jesus Christ, with patience only God could display, asked them only one question that kept ringing in their ears: "What do you think of Christ?"

The effect of this question has gone way beyond the Temple walls, beyond Israel's borders. This question has traveled the entire globe, and it is knocking on every window, every door, every heart.

What do you personally think of Christ? Do you know the real Christ? The Christ that has not been conditioned by today's preachers of morality? The Christ that has not been reduced to the service of political parties? Not the Hollywood one, not the literature-portrayed one, not the Greek Orthodox or the Catholic one? But the real one — God's Christ?

The One in Whose eyes our status before God was hopeless — destined for eternal hell? The One Who of His own free will and inconceivable love assumed human flesh forever to achieve for us the standard of righteous human life and to pay for our sins with it? The One in Whose resurrection and ascension are hidden all our future, all our hope, all our strength and justification?

The Christ who calls on those perishing, who forgives the lawless, who fills with meaning the lives of the desperate? The Christ to Whom not only your sin has been given, but also your life? Christ the Savior and Lord?

There is no other.

Christ is not an idea, not a brand. He is a Person waiting for your clear and unambiguous answer to the question, "What do you think of Christ?"

The answer to this question has the power to alter eternity for your soul and alter your earthly life as well. The answer to this question is not a formality. The consequences of your choice will sooner or later become obvious for everyone — for you, God, and those around you.

Perhaps you know much about Christ, and this book added just a fraction to your intellectual treasure. The issue is not whether you know much of God or little. As we have already mentioned, God is exceedingly greater than all our intellectual abilities. The issue is what you are in relation to Him — an outside observer, or a son?

Just like I promised on the cover of this book, no matter how much you knew already about God and religion, this brief book will forever change your perception of Christ and what He has done for you. It will either bring you to dedicate your life to God on a deeper level — expressed in repentance, practical living in unity with Jesus Christ, and following His teaching. Or, like the Pharisees who understood clearly that they were dealing with God in the flesh, it will cause you to crucify Him again. What you think of Christ will make all the difference in your life. It will also make all the difference after you die.

WHAT DO *YOU* THINK OF CHRIST?

- What is Biblical salvation? From what or whom do you need to be saved?

- How are you hoping to obtain salvation?

- Would you be willing to give the person dearest to you for the salvation of criminals? What conclusions do you arrive at as you realize that God took this step for your salvation?

- What motivates you to live a godly life?

ABOUT AUTHOR

Alexey Kolomiytsev is the senior pastor, serving a bilingual congregation at Word of Grace Bible Church in Battle Ground, Washington. He is the president of the Word of Grace International Ministries, focused on training ministers and teaching the Bible to reach Slavic people worldwide.

Alexey is a frequent speaker at conferences in the USA and abroad, and the author of numerous books and articles, translated into multiple languages. He is the most impactful Reformed expository preacher in the Slavic world nowadays.

Alexey holds two masters degrees in theology and is married to Tatyana, who has become a faithful friend and assistant in the ministry.

WORD OF GRACE INTERNATIONAL MINISTRY
Truth That Transforms Lives

The aim of our ministry is to make the preaching of the Word of God, clear and authoritative, available to all Russian-speaking people in the world. The ultimate goal of our efforts is the salvation of sinners and life transformation of Christians. We use two principal methods towards this purpose: the Bible Institute, which equips God's people with a deep knowledge of Scripture and its practical application, and the Media Ministry, which conveys the truth about God using modern, easily accessible technologies.

This ministry operates on the basis of Word of Grace Bible Church in Battle Ground, WA. We thank the Lord that currently, it is a source of help and blessings for millions of Russian-speaking people worldwide.

If you are a person that not only loves the truth, but eagerly wishes to share it with others, partnering with the Word of Grace International Ministry is a wonderful opportunity. Please pray for the spread and work of God's word in the hearts of people. We would also be grateful for financial support of the ministry at www.slovo.org/ministry. You may also write out a check to:

> Word of Grace International Ministries
> 1317 NE 12th Ave,
> Battle Ground, WA 98604
>
> Our contacts: +1 360. 977. 2182
> infomedia@slovo.org
> www.preciouschrist.org